Advance Praise

"In her new collection of essays, *Including the Periphery*, Roselee Blooston's humanity, heart, and honesty are on full display. Whether she's discussing her excitement over publishing her first book, her grief after the death of her husband, or her complicated feelings about her mother, she opens the doors of her life for her readers. And we, the readers, are the better for it!"

> — Deborah Kalb, author of *Off to Join the Circus* and other books

"In this her fifth book, *Including the Periphery*, a collection of personal essays, Blooston takes us with her through the years. In writing that is candid and consistently engaging, she shows us the budding self-reliance of her youth, the gifts and pressures of her life as a teaching artist, writer, wife and mother, and the relationships and connections she nurtures and basks in now in her later years. She doesn't hide from us the pain and loneliness of having to start over after her beloved husband's untimely death but neither does she stay there or apologize for her steady movement forward. At the completion of this vibrant yet understated book, you'll feel as if you've experienced a nearly full picture of a life well-lived. You'll not only enjoy Blooston and admire the meaning she's made of her life thus far, you'll also find yourself hoping you're creating as good a version of it for yourself."

— Maria Giura, author of *Celibate: A Memoir* and *What My Father Taught Me*

"A moving, beautifully written essay collection exploring the arc of a creative woman's experience. With intelligence, wit, and candor, Blooston traces her journey from adolescent inexperience to hard-won wisdom, exploring milestones of marriage, motherhood, widowhood, her son's nuptials, and her embrace of writing as a healing expression of identity and creativity. These essays are deeply personal yet universal in their exploration of love, loss, and the possibility of reinvention. Read this book and cheer for her resilience, a reminder that the examined life is well worth living."

— Nancy Gerber, author of *Burnt Toast: A Memoir of My Immigrant Grandmother*

"Writing with a perspective gained over seven decades, Roselee Blooston comes to terms with a series of life's disappointments with grace and fortitude. Her fifth book and second memoir, *Including the Periphery*, is a chronological series of personal essays spanning from her teenage years to present day. Readers will feel they are peeking into Blooston's private journals as she shares intimate details of her life and will learn how this resilient author has found joy in a sometimes-challenging world."

— Dian Seidel, author of *Kindergarten at 60: A Memoir of Teaching in Thailand*

Including the Periphery

Personal Essays

Including the Periphery

Personal Essays

Roselee Blooston

Apprentice House Press
Loyola University Maryland

Author's Note: Out of respect for the privacy of certain individuals, I have occasionally used initials rather than names.

An early version of "Shadow Career" was published online by Burning Bush Publications in 2001.

"The W Word" was originally published online in *Midcentury Modern Magazine* in 2016.

Aspects of "Not Penelope Anymore" appeared in *Dying in Dubai*, published in 2016 by Apprentice House Press.

"Writing Life" was first published as blogs on my website (roseleeblooston.com) in 2016 and 2017.

"Upkeep" was inspired by Nora Ephron's "On Maintenance" in *I Feel Bad About My Neck* (New York: Alfred A. Knopf, 2006), p.31-49

First Edition

Casebound ISBN: 978-1-62720-612-9
Paperback ISBN: 978-1-62720-613-6
Ebook ISBN: 978-1-62720-614-3

Printed in the United States of America

Design by Apprentice House Press
Editorial Development by Olivia DiTroia
Author Photograph taken by Maureen Gates

Published by Apprentice House Press

Apprentice
House Press
Loyola University Maryland

Loyola University Maryland • 4501 N. Charles Street, Baltimore, MD 21210
410.617.5265 • www.ApprenticeHouse.com • info@ApprenticeHouse.com

Also by Roselee Blooston

Dying in Dubai
Trial by Family
The Chocolate Jar and Other Stories
Almost: My Life in the Theater

For my friends

The unexamined life is not worth living.
—Socrates

Just get up and dance.
—Martha Graham

Contents

Introduction

This collection has been compiled over many years and ranges in subject and era from adolescence to my seventies. Read in order (though that is not required) the loosely linked set of personal essays offers variations on recurring themes involving change, perspective, and renewal. Together, they can be taken as companion pieces—an informal sequel—to my first memoir, *Dying in Dubai*.

I examined an early health crisis, a stalled teaching career, distorted vision, marriage as Greek myth, widowhood, and the writing life. I chronicled my return to a haunted vacation spot, my wedding through the lens of my son's nuptials, as well as late-life dating, upkeep's vicissitudes, and the delivery of end-of-life wishes. I also explored the significance of reunions, of an enduring recipe, and of the landscape around my Hudson Valley home. Throughout, my point of view and priorities evolved. After decades of tunnel vision, I have learned to include the periphery, allowing the past to inform the present, but not to overwhelm it. I trust that the resulting pages will resonate with readers of all ages.

Puberty

I was a late bloomer. I didn't get my period until I was thirteen, almost fourteen. It was summer, and I had just come home from day camp. My parents were very protective and wouldn't let me or my younger brother or sister attend sleep-away camp. They preferred to keep us close.

For the previous seven summers, I had attended Webster-Neal, a camp run by the Marjorie Webster Junior College in Washington, D.C. on its lush green campus. The counselors were all women, students who intended to become physical education, or music, or art, or elementary school teachers. I loved them. However, this was my eighth and last year. Enough was enough. I was a teenager after all. I would miss swimming lessons, archery, hula hoops, baton and ribbon twirling, and arts and crafts, not to mention the friends I met, most of whom had already graduated to independent summer experiences. I missed them and knew it was time for me to move on too.

I stepped off the camp bus and into the sultry atmosphere of our house. We didn't have central air conditioning, only window units in my parents' bedroom and our playroom. The attic fan helped a little, but not much. Washington, D.C. and its adjacent suburbs—we lived in Maryland—were humid in August. Very. The city had been a swamp long before it became the nation's capital.

Every afternoon, my younger siblings—my brother and sister—and I would wait for the sound of the ice cream truck chiming down our hilly street. Then we'd run outside, nickels and dimes in hand, to buy an ice-cold treat. We'd lick our popsicles and ice cream cones, lapping up a sweet reprise from the oppressive air around us.

But one August afternoon I missed the cold snack because I was in the upstairs bathroom staring at my underwear, which was stained a rusty salmon. I knew what it meant. My mother had endlessly prepared me with long talks, and lectures about women's bodies.

Mother handed me a pad—a "sanitary napkin," as it was called—which in those days was a bulky cottony rectangular thing with long ends that had to be looped through a garter belt and secured front and back so that the pad wouldn't slip and leak. If it did, the result was *un*sanitary: a condition according to my cleanliness-obsessed mother that would be shameful. I left the bathroom, in shock at the realization that from this moment on I was "a woman."

Mother greeted me with, "Now you can get pregnant. No intercourse until your wedding night." She never said "sex," only "intercourse." Though she had said this dozens of times before, this pronouncement in the context of my official entry into womanhood had much more weight than all the previous admonitions put together. I had been primed to fear sex; now I was terrified.

Mere days later, Mother handed me *Ideal Marriage: Its Physiology and Technique* by Theodoor Hendrick van de Velde, a Dutch gynecologist. The book was published in 1926, a year before my mother was born. It was 1965, and there had been a revised edition out that year, but the copy my mother gave me must have been the one her mother gave her, because its pages were yellow, and the binding was broken. Nevertheless, this had been the best-known guide to sex for decades, an international best seller.

For the next couple of weeks, I sat on a lounge chair outside, despite the relentless heat, and read. Somehow, I couldn't bear to read the book indoors, as if the walls would force me to face myself in the act of growing up or as if the information was a dirty secret that needed sunlight to disinfect it. Most of the contents were over my head, but I dutifully studied the anatomical diagrams of male and female anatomy and tried to absorb the book's overarching message of erotic equality, that both men and women deserve a pleasurable sex life throughout their marriages. Said pleasures were described by the author in detail, including foreplay, positions, and orgasm, which I imagined as a spectacular sunset bursting light and color throughout my body—a dead-on intuitive leap, however trite, for a girl who hadn't yet experienced one. My teenage understanding was intellectual and imaginative. My mind took in the information and stored it for later; my body wasn't close to being ready to take on the activities delineated.

To be clear, my mother was no prude, at least not concerning her own erotic life. In my teens and twenties, she told me far too much about her sex life with my father. She was very proud of how orgasmic she was. "I'm multi-orgasmic," she'd proclaim, as if she'd won a contest. I'd stare at her dumbfounded. I was expected to listen, marvel, but not to participate. She swung wildly between asserting a Victorian standard for her daughters and a sixties/seventies second wave feminist standard for herself. To her, it seemed, I was still a child. There could be only one woman in the house, and she was that woman. This shut me down for years, though I allowed my urges what reign I could give them—make-out sessions, necking, petting, first base, second base—and eventually, masturbation for relief.

The following summer after ninth grade, my last year in junior high, as we called it, I went shopping with my mother in downtown Washington at Garfinckel's, a high-end department store that catered to the upper middle class, and as far as my mother was concerned, had the best merchandise in the area. I didn't enjoy shopping the way Mother did. She couldn't get enough of it. I think because she grew up with little, the ability to pick and choose and buy meant everything to her.

She didn't believe in sales or discounts; according to her, the reduced price indicated the inferiority of the goods. Absurd now, of course, but then, it was her gospel. The more she paid for an item, the better she believed it to be. I took high-end shopping for granted; it was no big deal to me—a bore rather than a quest. Years later, when I struggled to support myself as a teacher, I guiltily surveyed sales racks for a bargain. In doing so, I was betraying Mother's creed, but as a teenager tagging along, I just wanted to get what we came for and leave.

We did, but not the way I wanted. Mother and I were in the perfume aisle on the first floor and suddenly, I got woozy and faint. I didn't black out, but my mother, alarmed, rushed me into a taxicab—she didn't drive—and over to the emergency room of the George Washington University Hospital, where fourteen years earlier, I had been born.

The resident who examined me, told me that I had beautiful eyes. His were dreamy too. They were marine blue and his open unlined face exuded kindness. If this doctor had had a full head of hair, I would have figured that he was in his twenties, but he was balding, so I surmised that he was more than twice my age, thirty at least. No matter, I had an instant crush on him. Mother noticed. "You like him, don't you?" she whispered, when he left the cubicle. She was trying to distract me. I nodded, still feeling dizzy.

When the doctor returned, he told us not to worry—the tests had all checked out. "It's probably hormonal," he said, i.e., related to my period, and sent me home to rest. By this time, my father had appeared. His law office was downtown; he had hopped in a cab as soon as my mother called. He looked pale. He knew himself well enough not to drive, though unlike my mother, he could have. Any threat to the welfare of his family sent him down a dark path, which would have compromised his concentration on the road. He was the sole survivor of his Polish Jewish family, the only one to make it out before Hitler marched in. He built a new life in America, married my mother, had three children, and a successful career as an attorney, but the fear that it was all fragile and could vanish in an instant dogged him.

"Are you okay, Rosie?" He was the only person who called me that. I found the diminutive comforting. Then he kissed me on the forehead. I nodded, though my head still spun like a merry-go-round. I couldn't speak because I was embarrassed at causing such concern. I had learned growing up in my isolated nuclear family that I was expected to behave well, not complain, and above all, not cause my parents—especially my father—worry of any kind. Even if I wasn't okay, I had to be, for him.

That evening and for the following two months, I spent most of my time in bed. Whenever I got up to go to the bathroom or to eat, the floor undulated beneath my feet. Mother took me to the pediatrician. I was still under his care, despite having turned the corner into adulthood. He sent me to various specialists. None of them found anything wrong with me. By the end of this eight week stretch, back in my childhood doctor's office, and feeling increasingly foolish as I walked into the examining room past fidgety kindergarteners, the doctor suggested to my mother that perhaps I should see a psychiatrist.

She said nothing to the doctor, but when we returned home, she sat me down at the kitchen table and pinned me with the stare that meant there could be no possible argument. "You heard the doctor. There's nothing wrong with you. When you come home from school, take a nap if you're tired. If you are feeling weak, sit down. You may always be fragile," —she said the last word like it was an unforgivable vice—"but you'll have to learn how to take care of yourself. I don't want to hear any more about how you are feeling." That last word, a sneer.

For Mother, the very mention of psychiatry had triggered her deepest fear: that her child wasn't normal, and that she was to blame. It's hard to conjure now in our therapized culture, but sending a child to a therapist or "shrink," was unacceptable to many parents in the sixties. My father, an immigrant, and my mother, a daughter of divorce, rendering her alien to many of her peers, were united in their belief that only they could solve their children's mental and emotional problems, albeit by wishing them away. To be fair, mothers were usually blamed for any problems with their children. My mother's reputation in the community had been, to that point, unimpeachable, and her three brilliant, well-behaved children were the reason. I could not be the one to ruin it. I got up from the table, went back to my room and shut the door, wondering how I would manage my unreliable body and confused mind.

At the end of the summer, with tenth grade in a new

school—the big public high school, Bethesda Chevy Chase—looming, Mother took me shopping once again, this time for school clothes. I'd been wearing pajamas exclusively since the incident in Garfinckel's. Now we were back, as if to replay and correct the scene, make it something benign and uneventful. I hadn't put on the training bra—training what I wondered? —she had bought me there that spring, when my first buds appeared on my almost flat chest. In the dressing room, I had submitted to the tape measure wielded by the cheery and efficient bra saleswoman, who had recommended a "starter" bra, the other name for trainer. Both words implied some agency on my part, and not a process out of my control. Now it didn't fit.

Once again, the saleswoman wrapped a measuring tape around my chest. "Well," she said, "you're not a starter anymore!" She was excited, as if I had achieved a major feat. "Two inches. You've grown two inches."

For a second, I thought she meant height. Wishful thinking from my five-foot self. Then she ran out of the dressing room. She came back with an assortment of lacy bras—real bras this time. My mother looked at me and smiled.

In the taxi on the way home, a full shopping bag in hand, I smiled too. That cute doctor had been right. My symptoms had been about puberty. For two months, my hormones had surged, short-circuiting every other system, putting me flat on my back. My body had needed all my energy to mature. As if reading my mind, mother said, "So many doctors, and it was the first one who knew what he was looking at. You were having a growth spurt. No wonder you were tired." I pictured myself as a cartoon character whose breasts suddenly ballooned into red and yellow bosoms, and I wanted to giggle. Then she said, not looking at me, but straight ahead at the road, "I'm sorry. I was too hard on you. I just didn't know what to do."

"It's okay, Mom," I said, holding up the bag. "I'm going to be okay now."

It took another year for the symptoms to subside completely. Although we knew and agreed that what had happened wasn't in my head, I had so internalized my mother's previous admonition to *act normally* no matter how I was feeling, that I didn't tell her when the occasional wave of dizziness or fatigue hit. Instead, I behaved according to the original plan: naps, lounging, behaving as if I was fine. And then I was.

The summer after my sophomore year, on the anniversary of the emergency room visit, my father took me on a vacation to Rehoboth Beach, Maryland. Mother's idea. It was the first time I went on a trip alone with my dad. The next time would be for college visits. I felt very grown up on the beach in my zebra-striped bikini and wearing my prettiest dresses at dinner in the glass-front dining room of the hotel.

By the time I went off to the Interlochen Arts Academy to study drama for my senior year, neither I nor my parents thought that I was fragile. They wouldn't have let me go if they had. The changes I had gone through strengthened me. It wasn't only my chest that was bigger, but my sense of self too. I could get through things.

Growing was ordinary. Everyone grew. But I experienced puberty as a sudden, propulsive shift, not only in how I looked, but also in how I felt. During this volatile time, I was tested. *Was I strong or weak? Was I ready to handle myself in the world? Could I overcome a physical challenge? An emotional one? Could I keep my own counsel?* I passed and stopped seeing my parents and other adults as all-knowing. The one exception was Doctor Blue Eyes, my first big crush, my first sensation of desire, because he saw me and knew what he was looking at: a young woman in development.

Shadow Career

I left my adjunct teaching job, which I had held for eight and a half years, in May 2000. It had been over long before that. When I took the position in the winter of 1992, I was filling in for an adjunct who had, after seven years, secured a fulltime position at a different university. I didn't want that. I had a three-year-old at home and a burning desire to pursue my acting career. At any rate, I'd been this route before. In the late seventies, a year out of grad school, I'd gotten a coveted tenure-track position with the University of Texas at Austin's drama department. My three years there were an important experience, but as gifted as I was academically, I wasn't an academic at heart. I turned down another higher ranked position, one at Virginia Military Institute—they had a very forward-thinking drama department then— landed my first professional acting job and with it my Actors' Equity Association card. So, I packed my bags for

New York City. I figured that I could always teach again someday.

Montclair State (then College, now University) was a ten-minute walk from home. The job took two mornings a week and demanded nothing else—no faculty meetings and no obligations other than teaching two acting classes. As the department chair said apologetically, he couldn't very well ask me to do more than the minimum, since the salary ($400 per credit hour, $1200 per course, $2400 total) was embarrassingly low. He assured me that the department was extremely loyal to adjuncts—they were never fired—and pointed to my predecessor's long, pardon the irony, tenure. I accepted the offer. I was happy to have something respectable to do that fit my son's schedule and that didn't demand too much. I figured I'd be there for two years, three tops.

But at some point, during my third year, I realized that I was working in a dream world. I had been lulled by the cordial faculty, the simplicity of the demands, the freedom to juggle other teaching and acting work, and above all, by the respect and admiration of my students. They didn't care if I was *only* an adjunct. They called me "Professor" anyway. Except to the students and a couple of real professors, I was invisible, my presence on campus negligible. I thought that was my fault. If I could make myself indispensable, maybe I'd have a shot at a fulltime job; job security meant more to me in my thirties than it had in my twenties.

With that in mind, I began to get more involved by showing up for the non-required faculty meetings. I was met with puzzled, *Haven't I seen you in the hallway? Did the department hire someone new?* stares. No other adjuncts came to these meetings.

A couple of years later, the department began to include me in "special projects" and planning sessions for the B.A. theater program for which I represented the entire acting division. They must have thought that if I was still around, I could be counted on. I was skilled, professional, and reliable. When the chair, who was also the head of the B.F.A. acting division, asked me to substitute for her in her senior Acting IV class, while she was on leave, I was flattered. I had, and still have, great respect for her and knew that it was mutual. I had been in a rut teaching B.A.s and non-majors only. This was a shot in the arm. *Wasn't teaching pre-professionals what I had trained for?* Well, not exactly. I had trained to become an actress. Never mind.

Of course, the new duties did not come with more pay, only more work, including longer class hours, an extra load of papers, and required attendance at hours of end-of-semester juries. Don't get me wrong. I enjoyed teaching the class and my new responsibilities, but the college was pulling a fast one: getting professorial skills for an adjunct salary.

The one time I asked for a raise, I was politely but firmly turned down. It wasn't the department's fault. The university was part of the New Jersey state system, and it had no respect for adjuncts. As far as the state was concerned, we were a cheap and easy solution to maintaining fiscal stability, because our employment offered no raises and no benefits except for a meager pension. It also conferred no status. At the introductory departmental meeting with the new president of the university, to which I was uncharacteristically invited, we took turns introducing ourselves around the table. As soon as I said that I was an adjunct, she looked right through me.

In 1996, I faced my stagnation. With three simultaneous part-time jobs, I was stuck on a non-career path. I applied to colleges and universities by the dozens, even to schools I couldn't commit to geographically. The chair gave me a glowing recommendation. During the two years I spent sending out my credentials, I got two responses and no interviews. At forty-four, I was too old and had been off the tenure track far too long. Adjunct work, I reasoned, would keep me relevant; then it turned into a gigantic detour, a road from which I could no longer turn back, a road to nowhere.

By the time I left Montclair State, I was one of three "professors" in the B.A. division who handled all B.A. theater majors and B.A. juries. I created and taught a special workshop for juniors on how to create and develop original performance material—a perfect merger of my acting, writing and solo performance background. My relationship with the department was at its peak. I had been there so long that I wasn't angry anymore. I accepted the job for what it was. In exchange for my patient, mature, and realistic attitude, I got all the trappings of a career and none of the perks. I was a permanent part-timer, in residence longer than some full-time professors.

On the one occasion when I thought of applying for a tenure track position, I held back. I knew from watching people come and go that the university was not inclined to hire adjuncts for full-time positions. Ever. I had been willing to be categorized as non-tenure track and would always be labelled as such.

I believed that the most important question for institutions of higher learning to address was not *what about the adjuncts?* but *what about the students?* The repercussions for them were serious. In an understaffed full-time faculty like Montclair State, which had more adjuncts in the theater department than full time professors, the students had fewer instructors to go to for guidance. Though I made myself available for extra coaching and career/ life advice, I was on campus only two half days a week. This was not an honest bargain. Universities promised full-time supervision and delivered a patched-together network of transient workers whose hearts and minds might be in the right place, but who were not given the means to support students with what they most needed: a consistent, stable faculty able to offer reliable counsel in their chosen majors. My shadow career became their shadow education, and that wasn't fair to anyone.

Ultimately, what prompted me to leave wasn't the money or lack of status. A newly formed adjunct union had increased my pay by fifty percent, and I was as much a part of the department as an adjunct could be. The truth was that after years of dead-end work and no way back into the full-time college teaching world, I was burned out. I cared about my students. Seeing them blossom in an art form I loved was a true pleasure. But after eight years, I knew that I was only a shell of the dynamic teacher I had once been. I had outgrown my teaching roots. I was going through the motions and that wasn't good enough for them or for me. My students deserved better. In the end, I left in the best possible way, not out of hurt or disappointment, but to embrace a new venture as the founding director of a local non-profit for writers.

In the spring of 2000, I walked into the chair's office to declare my intentions. He seemed to anticipate what I was going to say before I spoke. "Well," he said, leaning back in his swivel chair, "we always knew this day would come." After a few heartfelt words about how much I'd be missed, he proceeded to think out loud about how to cover my fall classes. I was being replaced before I was out the door.

That evening, at home, my husband asked, "How did it go?" I cried, surprising both him and me. It was an ending, albeit of my own choosing. I would miss the students and the few faculty members I had grown to know. I had also faced the delusion that I was irreplaceable. Then I got over it. Even so, I had to also face my part in this entire trajectory. That realization took much longer.

Thank goodness none of those mid-life tenure track positions had come through; I wouldn't have been able to sustain them, because they weren't true to my deepest intentions. For better or for worse, I had a calling, and it wasn't teaching. The instructional jobs I took for money, weren't jobs I internalized as "my career." In my inner monologue, they were minor gigs, "adjuncts" to my core self-image. Paradoxically, the work I did for love—acting and writing—which earned only sporadic cash, felt far more central to who I was than any regular paying position. Part-time university teaching provided the thin cover of respectable employment that I thought I needed to justify my creative projects—a sop to conventional societal demands, which gave me permission to do as I pleased. After I removed that cover and faced myself, I no longer needed it. My art *was* my career because I took it more seriously than any other endeavor. It was the sun to my adjunct responsibilities, forever casting them in the shade, where, I had to admit, I wanted them to stay.

my obligations. Thankful that the work could be
done and what the extent to which I... I became...
gratitude from persons to who I was than a day for...
the writing produced, the time spent and, because my
visited the full force of a... most unhappy, and that
a thought... to... plain representative portrait — I beg
to... had seen certain... which have made...
I... it was... known... they grieved and that over
and over as yet I am somewhat helps... that to settle
... that... it has seem... consoled than any short...
and say... is... the... as I... time... and...
lived... I had... as in what... so ... lovable... child...

Including the Periphery

I followed the tight-rope walker's credo: look straight ahead and know there could not possibly be any other way. After pursuing several passions, only partially ful-filled, I decided to start a non-profit for writers and envi-sioned the local literary community flocking to my door, along with loads of support for my own writing. I gave it everything except its name. For that I trusted Jerry, my ad man husband, to come up with something intriguing. He didn't disappoint: Tunnel Vision Writers' Project.

One usually thinks of "tunnel vision" as bad—see-ing only what's in front of you, zooming in too closely, no peripheral vision. But I knew better. Tunnel Vision also implied the monastic concentration of the artist, the single-mindedness necessary to produce great work. Shut the world out and focus! I'd lived my artistic life this way, and now the path had brought me to a public epiphany. By naming my new venture "Tunnel Vision" I was validating my entire belief system.

But my tunnel vision about "Tunnel Vision" was a problem. The negative connotations of the phrase had greater power than I could have ever imagined. Miguel Ruiz in *The Four Agreements* said, "Be impeccable with your word." I thought he just meant be polite. It wasn't until much later—after I was diagnosed—that I realized the insidious force of something as simple as a name.

It was June. TVWP's fifth year had been particularly hectic. I plowed from one demanding event to another—readings, workshops, collaborations—like organizing wedding upon wedding. Not that I'd ever organized a wedding, other than my own modest one, but in my bleary middle of the night panic over the myriad details involved in making our concert-reading-show happen, it's what I imagined wedding planning to be—an exhausting nightmare and I was the mother of every bride. As soon as the last performance ended, I dragged myself home and collapsed. Lying on my couch, gazing at the roses the cast had given me, I wondered how I had gotten into this position—in charge of everything, delegating almost nothing, and unpaid to boot. Of course, the answer was obvious. I'd done it to myself. I knew the signs of mental exhaustion; I'd been there before. This time though, the fatigue was deeper, more pervasive than being tired of teaching. Perhaps because this wasn't a job; it was *a mission*.

The next two weeks I made lame attempts at relaxation. I went swimming and out to lunch with girlfriends but singing in my ear was the constant hum of my "job." Amidst preparations for our fall offerings, I also had to diffuse the nutty demands of a playwright who insisted that I send back all her scripts. I tried to explain that we keep a copy of everything we produce for our archive. She couldn't understand the concept and bombarded me with certified letters demanding the return of "all copies." So, I proceeded to Xerox her script and send the "copy," along with the definition of copyright, and a pledge to never again "copy, distribute, publish or perform your work." Just as I typed my "sincerely yours," furious at this waste of my time and energy, it happened.

My right eye slammed shut.

At first, I thought that I'd gotten something in it—maybe a bug or a piece of dust. I ran to the sink to splash water on my face, but it still wouldn't open unless I closed my left eye first. The only way I could keep both eyes open at once was to look down at the floor; as soon as I tried to focus on an object in front of me, my eyes wouldn't work together.

I *need rest*, I thought. It must be eyestrain: all those hours on the computer compiling mailing lists, writing press releases, designing flyers, posters, brochures, and program bios—the long egotistical ones, mine included, and the short overly modest ones—not to mention my own writing, hard labor over long short stories. So, I took more time off—no computer, very little reading or writing, days by the pool. Nothing worked.

Weeks went by. I'd wake up in the morning and tell myself to stay still and to open my eyes slowly. *Look at the ceiling.* Good. *Look out the window.* Good. *Focus on the closet door, the photos of my son dotting the pale pink wall of my bedroom.* Good. *Now sit up.* I'd take a deep breath and close my eyes as if I were about to jump into very cold water. *Now open.* I'd open my eyes together and let out a short high breath, a sort of half Lamaze. I'd blink once. The right eye would lag a nano-second behind the left and then open. I'd slide out of bed and lower myself onto the adjacent sofa. This became a familiar ritual of slow, even movements, and quiet adjustments, ever since the disturbing day when I went from normal sight to one-eye blind. That was how I thought of it, though three ophthalmologists disagreed.

"Your sight is perfect," said the bald sixty-year-old specialist.

"It's probably an allergy," said the second, a cocky young guy with too much mousse in his hair.

"Dry eye," said the third, a spiffy dresser with a Toulouse Lautrec tie, who handed me a packet of artificial tears.

I had cried buckets through my college years, my favorite stress-reliever. Almost thirty years later, in my mounting desperation, this, unlike the other diagnoses, seemed plausible. Perhaps my eyes had finally run out of tears.

A month passed and the drops had fixed nothing. My eyes watered almost constantly, and I couldn't stand any kind of bright light. *They're all quacks,* I thought, as I tried in vain to close my left eye to let the right one see a little. Each morning, I looked at myself in the mirror, my face seized up with tension. The lines on the bridge of my nose, just above my brows and under my right eye, dug their way across my face. Every day the wrinkles deepened.

"I'm sending you to a neurologist," my GP said.

I appreciated his willingness to admit that he was stumped. But then little alarm bells went off. *Tumor? Stroke?* A friend of mine had been diagnosed with MS a few years ago and had problems with her eyes. No, it can't be. But one fact was undeniable: I had graduated from a minor problem to a major one. Something might be wrong with my brain.

This terrifying possibility and my constant anxiety over my fledgling organization kept me wide awake. *What if I couldn't raise the money to keep Tunnel Vision going? What if it had to fold? What if I wanted it to?* I was very proud of Tunnel Vision Writers' Project, Inc., but the world of a start-up non-profit was always unstable. I had driven myself relentlessly in the past five years. My efforts never seemed to be enough. Tunnel Vision was always strapped, and I, its chief engine, and full-time unpaid volunteer director, was running out of steam.

"Don't anticipate. It's probably nothing," Jerry said, referring to the next day's appointment with the neurologist.

"But I can't keep my eye open! I'm *driving* with one eye, for Christ's sake. I almost hit a dog yesterday!"

The golden retriever had been just out of my left eye's line of vision. I knew it was irresponsible, driving in this condition, but I carefully limited my routes—no highways and no rush hour. I resolved to constantly move my head side to side to make up for the loss of the right side.

The by-product of this half-baked caution was letting my fifteen-year-old grow up a bit faster. That summer he had an internship in the city. Instead, of driving Oliver door to door, I drove him to the train station with instructions to call me when he got to Hoboken, when he left the station in the Village, and again when he reached the studio door twenty minutes later. In the afternoon I had him reverse the pattern. Ollie was thrilled with the freedom. I was depressed. My little boy didn't need me so much anymore.

"I can't go on like this. It's been three months!" I looked over at Jerry whose own eyes were already closed. "It'll be alright. Try to get some sleep." Jerry rolled over into a snore. The alarm clock flashed 2:30 a.m. I turned my whole head to look down with my working left eye at the sleeping husband on my right and fell asleep thinking of Cyclops.

The neurologist was a funny personable guy, a Jay Leno of brain specialists. He tapped my knee, my elbow, scratched my palms with pencils, did eye and memory tests. "Recite these numbers backward: ten, six, eight, twenty-seven."

"Twenty-seven, eight, six, ten," I answered, sweating with longstanding test phobia.

"Good," he said, "have a seat." He gestured to the chair in front of his desk and left. "I'll be right back."

I assumed the pause was for dramatic effect, since there was no need to break the exam into two parts; I was fully clothed. Or maybe he needed a coffee break. My right eye closed. The weirdest part of all these appointments had been my inability to *show* the doctors what was happening to me. Whenever they were in the exam room with me both eyes stayed open. As soon as they left, the right eye slammed shut.

Dr. Jay reentered, all smiles. "There's nothing wrong with your brain."

I exhaled.

"This may be a form of tic."

"A tic?" I bit my lip. Maybe it *was* all in my head.

"Are you under stress?" the doctor asked, almost chuckling.

I restrained my urge to layer on the sarcasm. *Stress, why do you ask? I've been walking around with one eye closed for four months and nobody knows why. You're the fifth specialist I've gone to. I can't read, write, drive with both eyes open. Stress? You think?* Instead, I told him, "I've had a lot of pressure at work this year."

"That could do it," he said, and twirled his pen in anticipation, I assumed, of writing yet another useless prescription.

But I had to ask, "Is there anything you can do?"

He smiled again in an adolescent facsimile of empathy. His comic charm had already worn off. "I could give you anti-seizure medication, but the side effects can be pretty extreme."

"Like what?"

"Anything from lethargy to catatonia." He laughed, expecting me, his studio audience, to laugh right along with him.

Instead, I pictured myself lying on my bed, drooling.

Dr Jay dropped the pen on his desk from a height of about a foot. "This sort of thing tends to resolve itself in six to eight weeks. Let's just wait it out."

As if you're going to wait with me. As if you're going to have to drive home in this condition. It's already been sixteen weeks, and it hasn't "resolved itself!"

"Thank you," I said as I rose to leave. *At least it's not a tumor.*

On the way home I called Jerry. As soon as I said "tic", he told me to "take it easy." He didn't get it, but neither did the doctors. I wanted to be relieved, but I wasn't. I wanted a simple explanation, but the tic diagnosis didn't convince me. Yes, I was under stress, but I'd done everything I could to combat it. What about all the naps I'd taken listening to guided imagery tapes? And the homeopathic drops a friend had recommended? I had relaxed, meditated, and rested all summer, and the problem just got worse. I was sure the doctor was wrong. *My condition wasn't emotional or psychological. It was physical.* And there wasn't a damn thing I could do about it.

Three weeks later, Tunnel Vision critique groups began their sixth season. The fiction group was at full capacity. I hadn't seen the old members for three months and the new ones had met me only once at a brief interview. I knew one thing for sure: they would all notice my eye. My face hurt from months of one-sided squinting. *I'm worn out,* I thought. I would have to say something.

That evening, as I launched into the guidelines of our work together, I tried not to focus too intently on any one person. The group—all women this year—sat in polite attention. Just as I was about to go into attendance requirements, always a sore point for stay-at-home moms and commuting career women alike, it happened. My eyelid dropped. I looked down at the floor. When I looked up, I tilted my head to the right as if to direct their gaze up and to my left.

Then I told them. "I'm having a problem," I said. "With my eye. That's why I'm squinting."

It occurred to me as the women murmured, "Sorry! /What's wrong? /That's terrible," or simply peered at me sympathetically, that most of them hadn't noticed anything odd until I'd pointed it out. Then, of course, after my admission, that was all they noticed. I cut short the rest of my remarks and somehow got through the first round of critiques. Usually I loved this part, but not this time. This time, I couldn't wait to get out of there.

As I packed my briefcase, one of the new writers approached me. A scattered, rather insecure woman who held back in the critiques and wasn't sure if she could submit her work to the group, she was nothing if not direct now.

"I know a behavioral optometrist," she said.

"A what?"

"A behavioral optometrist. He specializes in the functioning of the eye. He's a genius. A real miracle worker."

"Oh," I said. "Sure. I've been to three ophthalmologists already. I could use a miracle."

"I'll email you with his contact information," she said as she breezed out of the room. A few weeks later she dropped out of the group, but I knew by then that she hadn't crossed my path as a writer. She'd come as a messenger. Her work with me was done.

Dr. K's office stood in stark contrast to the previous doctors' offices I had blinked my way through that summer. Unlike their gleaming confrontationally white reception areas, this entryway was dark, a deep blue gray that immediately soothed. A wall-sized window behind the staff area provided most of the light. Ceiling fixtures were dim, lamps homey. I began to think of how sensitive my drop-filled eyes were during previous check-ups. Walking out into a harshly lit room always jarred me. Here the personable, completely unpretentious atmosphere comforted. It was a Saturday. There were no other patients in the waiting area. I was happy to be alone, unwatched.

"Roselee?" A white haired slightly balding man with a soft voice and extremely kind eyes motioned me down the hall and into his office. No intervening nurse. No office hierarchy. After we both sat, he asked, "What can I do for you?"

I explained the history of the past six months. I told him how frightened I was on the way to his office. I took the bus and subway, since driving was out of the question. As I navigated the underground tunnel connecting Times Square and Grand Central the rushing on-coming crowds wreaked havoc with my one-eye balance. I hugged the walls and stair railings.

He listened, took notes, and then said, "I'm going to give you a complete exam. We're going to take as long as necessary to get to the bottom of your problem. Now breathe."

Throughout the following he told me many times to "breathe" or "take a breath." He then proceeded from the familiar eye chart test, reestablishing my excellent eyesight, to new tests for depth perception and eye muscle function. Over and over, I watched various boxes and dots shift up and down in each eye's field of vision, then come together in the center, or not. He administered eye drops but never left the room.

After a forty-minute examination, he turned to me and said, "I see what's wrong. To focus properly, eye muscles must coordinate with and adjust to each other. Your eyes don't do that. You have 'drifting eyes.' Normal drift is zero to two. Yours is off the chart at eighteen."

I imagined my right eye shifting out the side of my head in a straight line eighteen inches from my ear.

Dr. K continued, "This means your eyes aren't working together. One closes because it can't focus with the other drifting back and forth."

"Both eyes are affected?" I asked.

"Yes."

"How did this happen? Why didn't any of the ophthalmologists catch it?"

Rather than trash his colleagues, he took the diplomatic route. "Eye doctors specialize in eye disease and tend to look at each eye in isolation. I'm an optometrist specializing in eye function, how eyes work together. You came to the right place."

I laughed and told him I was sent. Then I told him about Tunnel Vision.

He chuckled at the name and its possible psychosomatic effect. "The causes are many. But with no head injury in your history, I must ask, have you experienced a major loss in the recent past? One for which you did not properly grieve?"

I must have turned white.

"Are you alright?" he asked. "Would you like some water?"

"No. I'm okay." I was sweating and my hands had turned cold. "My father died two and a half years ago. His wife sued me and my siblings resulting in a jury trial. We won, but it took all the energy we had. Afterwards, I threw myself into my work. At first, I didn't have time to grieve, then I didn't *take* the time." I gulped and asked, "How could that affect my eyes?"

"I don't know how, but I do know that there is a connection between deferred grief and eye drift. You probably also have a weakness from your thyroid disease ten years ago, for which you have been compensating all this time. Tell me, when things get tough, what do you usually do?"

I hesitated, then answered, "I muddle through."

"Push through," he corrected. "You're rather a type A personality, aren't you?"

I wondered how he'd gleaned this from an eye exam in which I hadn't exactly taken charge, but I didn't doubt his reasoning. He'd nailed me.

I nodded and he continued. "After your father's death and subsequent strain, you pushed through the grief and stress for as long as you had to and then, this summer when you had a little time off, when you no longer *had* to function, your eyes finally de-compensated. You wouldn't slow down, so they did it for you."

I sat very still. This was both more than I'd bargained for and the perfect resolution to my struggle. There was something about this man—his directness, his stability—that allowed me to instantly accept the connection between my eyes and my loss, my visual distress and my spiritual pain. It isn't often that a stranger, let alone a doctor, sees you whole. Here was an optometrist diagnosing my unexpressed grief. My messenger was right: Dr. K was a benevolent genius. He had quite literally used my eyes as the windows to my soul. I had been wrong. My malady was emotional *and* psychological *and* physical after all.

"Is it curable?"

He smiled. "Yes. I will create a program of exercises for you. Vision therapy, here, at least once a week, for five or six months. I expect you will make a full and complete recovery."

Over-eager as usual, I did three sessions in the first ten days ending up with a splitting headache after the first hour. But once I got over fear of failing, the forty-five-minute sessions of computer games, 3-D glasses, balance board exercises, and speed-reading were fun. I loved the sense of accomplishment I got ascending from one level to the next.

Susan, my vision therapist, a warm and sensible woman, perhaps ten years older than me, acknowledged my "remarkable progress," but gently chided that my scores were sometimes *too* good, "hyper-normal."

Yes, I thought, I'm too old to be precocious. I had to learn to slow down.

"Breathe. Include the periphery," she'd remind me.

As I studied the 3-D picture of jungle trees, exotic flowers, and prowling tigers, I focused on a tiny monkey perched on a branch, and exhaled as my eyes took in the sky, leaves, ground, and animals, above, below, and on each side of the focal point.

"See the details around your focus. Always be aware of the whole picture."

The mantra worked its magic. The change was radical and immediate. By the second session I could drive again with both eyes open. Seeing without blinders meant taking in a dome-like picture with me at the center. At Susan's suggestion, I stuck red flags on either side of my computer. The screen became a window seen within a larger window, the room. By the third session, I was grounded, my balance restored.

I danced all night at my fiftieth birthday party with nary an errant blink.

Over the next few months, check-ups with Dr. K confirmed my progress, and helped me to profoundly alter my path. I began to understand the link between my eyes and my life. I stopped tunneling and broadened my view. I started to take care of myself and made some wrenching decisions. My non-profit had to be scaled way back. Since it wasn't a real job, I couldn't let it divert me from writing. I could no longer mother others at my own expense. Ironically, Tunnel Vision had both exacerbated my problem and provided a vehicle for its solution. Time to face my limitations. I couldn't single handedly run the organization I'd created. I couldn't honor my creativity by putting it last. Above all, I had to look deeply into my love and sorrow. The play about my father that I'd started when I founded TVWP, had to be finished. It's title, "Tikkun," in Hebrew meant spiritual repair.

Two years later, with the play complete, and the non-profit in the background, I focused on writing a novel about loss. My eyes weren't perfect, but I knew how to use them. And a hidden purpose in founding Tunnel Vision Writers' Project surfaced. I had needed something to stave off the emptiness I anticipated when my only son went off to college. Like my father's death, this loss couldn't be cheated; it had to be felt. When I saw my boy pass through the college's gates, surrounded by hundreds of other young men and women, weeping parents, and sympathetic tissue-bearing upper classmen, there I was—with both eyes open, watching him, my most cherished focal point, recede—simultaneously aware of my sadness and pride, my future with my husband, the leaves not yet fallen, my new freedom, and the sun brightly descending, all at once seeing the whole, including the periphery.

Not Penelope Anymore

In January 2007, my husband, Jerry, and I went dune busting in the desert surrounding Dubai with a dozen other tourists. He had been working there as a media consultant for the past two and a half years, returning to our home in New Jersey every couple of weeks. I found the schedule barely tolerable. It created constant tension between us, shaking the foundations of what had been an extremely close twenty-four-year partnership in which we embraced our traditional roles of provider husband and stay-at-home wife, while at the same time supporting our individual passions—his as a writer, kayaker, and preservationist; mine as an actress, teacher, and arts administrator. I held on through my loneliness, telling myself that this would end soon. It did. But not in the way I had hoped.

This was our second trip as a couple to the United Arab Emirates. In 2005 we had taken our college age son to the Dubai Film Festival. During that visit I had felt deeply unsettled by the strange intersection of over-the-top glamour and stifling repression that defined Dubai. Undercover police in traditional dishdashas manned our luxury hotel's lobby. Women in full-length burqas shopped in the high-end malls, carrying Fendi bags, their red-soled Louboutin's clicking on the polished floors. A hotel bellhop, face clouded by fear, backed out of our room after carrying our bags, refusing a tip. The atmospheric dissonance of this Rodeo Drive on Mars exhausted and confused me. Nature made sense. This city did not.

This time, when Jerry suggested that we join a desert tour, I welcomed the break, but my stomach churned from the jeep's wild trek up and down the dunes. At the dinner site, we sat on pillows under the stars to watch belly dancers and to feast on mezze, the Middle East version of tapas. The elemental beauty of sky, sun, and sand gave me a moment of serenity, the first since I had arrived. The setting sun's brilliance cast a rust and gold shadow over the sand, in stark contrast to the surreal metropolis we had left behind.

We lined up for a camel ride. I had my doubts. The animals reeked and were a good deal taller than I had envisioned. I was afraid of heights, including one between humps, where I would have to sit.

"Come on. It'll be fun. Great photo op," Jerry said. So up I went, gripping the saddle so tightly that my knuckles turned white. Luckily, the ride wasn't much, once around the makeshift sandy parking lot, and that was it.

"Smile," my husband said. Seeing his beaming face and goofy Kermit the Frog grin, how could I not? It was the smile I had fallen in love with at first sight, one rainy evening at a Manhattan bus stop. More than twenty years later, we had been through a lot: near financial ruin, his serious depression and drinking, a flirtation with one of his co-workers which sent us to couple's counseling, and the constant stress of leading separate lives. But at bottom, no matter what, he was my guy, and as our song went, *my one and only love.*

Near midnight, in the rickety bus on the way back to the city, Jerry whispered in my ear, "You're Penelope." He was referring to the long-suffering and faithful wife of Odysseus.

"Didn't she wait a decade for him to return?" I asked, bristling at the thought.

"Twenty years," he said.

I shook my head. "Don't think for one second that I'm going to do any such thing. I told you that four years was the limit, and I meant it." That early and somewhat arbitrary deadline, anchored by our son's time in college, felt like a biological clock ticking down the minutes until our separation would be over. Though a traditional wife and mother, once Jerry began traveling, I clung to my self-image as an independent person, at least in spirit, a label affixed by my parents, when I rejected elementary school cliques, and later among my peers in my stubborn adherence to a creative path. But living the reality of a long-distance marriage, I felt only my total, utter dependence.

"It might not be so easy to leave when you want me to," Jerry said. "It might take a couple more years to wrap things up." I realized that our situation was not on par with what military couples had to face, but I had little confidence that I could handle it if the current scenario became open-ended.

"You don't have a couple more years," I said, as if I knew that his life would end, when what I really meant was that our life together might. My husband compared my steadfastness to a mythic mate's, but its origins weren't noble, only part inertia, part fatigue.

Once, when I asked Jerry how he would characterize our marriage, he said, "We're entwingled." We laughed at the nonsense word, a definition that made perfect private sense, more playful than "enmeshed," less clinical than "co-dependent."

I couldn't laugh in that hotel bus. Jerry looked dead tired. I felt his untenable position, caught between my needs and his work. I stroked his hand and kissed his cheek. I hated that I had given him an ultimatum and wanted to lighten the mood. "So, if I'm Penelope and you're Odysseus, who are the sirens?"

Jerry smiled. "They're out there. But don't worry. I'm lashed to the mast." Then he put his head on my shoulder and fell asleep. I thought about the kiss he had exchanged with his assistant, how it had shocked and hurt me, and how we had moved on with renewed resolve to make this temporary situation work and not let anyone or anything come between us again.

But try as I might, I couldn't dismiss the comparison. My husband saw me as Penelope. Perhaps there was something to it. We each had one son. Our love for our husbands caused us pain, though neither of us gave up hope that they would return. But while she represented the most loyal mate imaginable, enduring two decades alone, I was fading at the three-year mark. Odysseus went off to war. My husband left to seek his fortune. Penelope had many suitors. To fend them off, she created a clever plan in which she would not hear their proposals until the shroud she wove by day for her father-in-law was done. At night she unraveled the day's work. I had no such suitors. Instead, I occupied myself with my writing, my girlfriends, my son, and plans for my husband's next trip home, all while my marital life unraveled like her handiwork.

I realized that war and time aside, Penelope and I were sisters. Long before Jerry came into my life, when I was still a virginal college girl, I was cast as another strong, resolute wife in the title role of "Lady Precious Stream," a play set in the Tang Dynasty, which had a great deal in common with Homer's tale, including war as the cause of separation, tempting suitors, and of course, lots and lots of waiting. I must have had, even then, the essential qualities of such a woman. But in an instant, life can change and so can meaning.

When, a year after our trip to the dunes, my husband was stricken with a brain aneurysm, my son and I flew to his side and watched him die in a Dubai hospital. Then and there I began to shed the Penelope in me, the waiting wife. *What was there to wait for after such a loss?* I had to admit, angry and frustrated as I had been by the apt comparison, I had also agreed to its terms when I married Jerry at the bus stop where we met. Our quirky nonconformist wedding belied our very conforming marriage. It must be said though, that he understood my sacrifice. While he was in Dubai, Jerry wrote me, via email, love letters.

I know you have paid a heavy price to stay by my side. But I want you to know that there isn't any future I can imagine without you. This path has been painful, but I know in my heart that there is no one for me other than you. And yes, I see us growing old and more in love as long, as I finally quit smoking. You are in my dreams tonight.

Unlike mine, Penelope's husband did not die. When Odysseus finally returned, disguised as a beggar, Penelope failed to recognize him, though he won every contest and slayed the suitors. Not until he told her a secret only the two of them knew did she believe he was her husband. Jerry and I had no such reunion. He did not come back to me whispering "entwingled" in my ear.

After his death, I did not recognize myself. I was no one's wife, no one's Penelope, faithfully honoring her vows, waiting for her errant husband to return. Rather, I waited for my essential self to resurface. When I entered a social gathering alone, I saw glimpses of the girl I was before marriage. I felt Jerry as a phantom limb and ached for him, but I also heard my voice holding court, not in Jerry's outsized convivial way but in my own more mea-sured style. Each mundane act we did together, that I now had to do alone—grocery shopping, walking the dogs, getting an oil change for the car, cooking dinner—rebuilt my autonomy. I worked hard to shed the remnants of my wifely role, the tendency to stoically tough out every hardship, to put myself last, and above all, to wait.

In my single state, except in relationship to my son, I put myself first. Without the person I turned to for ballast and perspective, I stopped taking on compromising situations and demanding people. I asked myself, "What's in this for me?" With Jerry, the answer was, "Everything." No longer. I became more selfish and healthier. At night in bed, moving center, banking myself with pillows on either side to replace the body that had once warmed me, I re-learned how to dream my own dreams. Married, I had been faithful to Jerry. Alone, I learned to be faithful to myself.

In the years since Jerry's death in Dubai, that city, which had been the setting and catalyst for wrenching change, became a larger metaphor for alienation from the truth. Its glittery surface hid a disturbing repressive underbelly. Ex-pats like my husband lost themselves in chasing its superficial promises of wealth and power. Menial laborers lost their freedom building its flashy skyscrapers and catering to its jet-set tourists. Wealthy wives shopped for designer clothes while fully veiled from the world's gaze. Their obvious constrictions must have demanded tremendous patience, cleverness, and strength. I began to see them as Penelopes, and I understood that my discomfort with Dubai was about more than the city's schizophrenic identity. Jerry and I could not have been the husband and wife we were in the United States in the U.A.E. We could not have supported each other's many needs and passions. My role there could only have been attendant spouse.

Eventually, I found the resources, inner and outer, to move away from our family home and into one of my own. I began a new chapter in the Hudson Valley where I knew no one—a fact I found more exhilarating than daunting. There were so many people to meet, so much to explore. The future would be a new adventure. My husband's death had rendered the myth of the patient wife a thing of the past. It had unmarried me, and since I had no intention of getting married again, I welcomed my new freedom. After all, despite the struggles and frustrations, I had been deeply satisfied by being Jerry's wife. That satisfaction sustained me. No longer waiting, I stopped following a restrictive marital script. I wrote my own. And in my new script, I was not Penelope anymore. I was Odysseus.

The W Word

A few months after my husband's death, I was in my gynecologist's office filling out forms. I worked my way down the page, checking boxes. *Are you a) married, b) single, c) divorced—* What would that have to do with the state of my vagina? I wondered—*or d) widowed?* My hand froze. So did my mind. Up until then, I hadn't thought of myself as a widow, though of course, others did.

During my dealings in the Middle East, I was referred to as "Jerry Mosier's widow"—not *me*, the woman who had kept her name, who considered herself an independent person—and not as "Mrs. Mosier," the conforming moniker I used there, while Jerry was alive. Overnight, my label had changed from "husband's property" to his *abandoned* property.

The form I had filled out many times in many doctors' offices brought me up short. I'd never noticed the last category, because I had, for almost twenty-five years, checked the first one. I wiped the sweat off my upper lip, stilled my shaking hand, and marked the box. I was now *officially* a widow.

The dictionary defines "widow" as "a woman who has lost her husband by death" especially "one who has not remarried." Putting aside "lost," which has always bothered me—I didn't misplace Jerry; he died—I found the last part most disturbing. I had no intention of remarrying. *Would I be, from now on, first and foremost a widow?*

Mere weeks into my mourning, I said to my closest friend, "I'm not married anymore. I'm single." I couldn't yet say the W word out loud. But "single" didn't accurately describe my new identity. It left out the marriage that had shaped my adult life. "Single" described my immediate state but ignored my marital history; only "widow" could describe that. I was alone and unattached, true, but not to my past. Memories of our life together—our meeting and marriage at a Manhattan bus stop, the birth of our only child the night before our third anniversary, our summers on Martha's Vineyard, our private silly games—meant everything to me, especially after the other repository of those memories was gone.

I didn't say "widowed" either. The verb's definition: "to cause to become a widow; to survive as the widow of; to be deprived of something greatly loved or needed," confirmed that something terrible had *happened to* me. Yes, I had been deprived of *someone* I greatly loved and needed, but I rejected the implied victimhood.

After the incident in the doctor's office, I needed to process my new awareness. One day while cleaning and sorting closets, which I did obsessively to control the chaos of grief, I climbed a ladder to reach the highest shelf in my bedroom closet where I had stored a childhood doll collection. There I found The Widow.

I hadn't thought of her as one, but in my situation it seemed obvious. She was dressed all in black, her head covered with a mantilla trimmed in black lace, her soft legs hidden in black stockings, her face moon white, her eyes unfathomable—the quintessential Italian widow, mourning inside her room with the curtains closed. She was creepy. But that hardly mattered. The minute I found her again, I brought her down and sat her on my bed, on my side, or what used to be my side—I'd been drifting center. She stood-in for me since I couldn't shut myself away, nor would have wanted to, though on a bad day that old-fashioned, isolated formal year of mourning made sense. With the doll in place, I didn't have to go to that extreme. I didn't like her—her sad, grieving vibe depressed the energy in the room—but I knew intuitively that I needed her in front of me every day.

As the year anniversary of my husband's death approached, I became impatient with the Widow. I wanted to evict her. I thought about relegating her to the closet again, but when the day came, I placed her in the yellow bag I used for giveaways and put her on the curb. I still mourned but couldn't look at her anymore. Later, I understood that choosing this figurative replacement was an act of deep-seated denial. *She* was The Widow. Not me. During and after that first year, I avoided saying anything about my circumstances. I desperately wanted to pretend I was ordinary and unscathed, and figured that, in any case, my miserable appearance made it obvious. I felt as if I had "W" tattooed on my forehead.

Sometimes I met with other longtime widows to compare notes, to learn how to navigate the world on my own. I didn't enjoy these encounters because I didn't want to identify with this sorrowful sisterhood. I couldn't join bereavement groups because I was unable to bear anyone's grief but my own. One of the widows had remarried—she was technically not a widow anymore—but said a part of her would always be her first husband's wife. Another told me how like my husband I would become. "You'll embody the qualities he gave you for ballast," she said. She was right. I'm more gregarious, chatting up everyone I meet and less afraid to say what I think, like blunt, gutsy Jerry. A third widow bummed me out with tales of predatory men—widows are assumed to have money—and pitying glances from friends and relatives. I'd gotten plenty of those, too. They made me cringe.

I realized that the pity in those glances reflected the societal shame attached to widowhood. In some cultures, widows are outcasts, driven from their homes, exiled, poor and alone, or worse, in the Hindu practice of sati, expected to immolate themselves on their husband's funeral pyre. In Dubai, under Sharia law, a widow cannot inherit her husband's money unless every male family member agrees in court to allow it. My lawyer and I spent a year trying to circumvent that law to extricate my husband's bank account. Like all women there, widows had no standing and no power apart from the men who controlled their lives, even from the grave.

In our more modern culture, widowhood's demotion in status manifests in subtler, yet unmistakable ways. At a dinner party given by an old friend, I was introduced to the husband of another woman. I smiled and shook his hand. His wife instantly inserted herself between us, declaring, "He's *my* husband." I backed away, startled. The hostess giggled at the bald, awkward moment. I was the spidery black widow spinning my web around her friend's man. Men I met often mentioned their wives immediately, letting me know *they're taken*. Both men and women assumed that I *must* be on the prowl, because a woman without a man is incomplete. There are more unattached people in the United States than ever before, but it's still a couples' world, and in that world widows are suspect.

I also felt my demotion in looks of pity by the plumber or the electrician, when they came into my new home to fix a leaking faucet or faulty outlet, and we made small talk, during which I noticed them wondering *Woman alone? No wedding ring?* I'd mention "my late husband," which felt wrong—Jerry was always on time—but conveniently indirect, since it described my husband, not me.

The workman would tilt his head sideways and frown in sympathy. Then he'd murmur, "I'm sorry," as if it had happened yesterday, not years ago.

"Thank you, I'm fine," I'd say too quickly, and he'd return to work tightening a washer or checking a breaker. *Good*, we'd both think, *got past that*.

Sometimes I'd say more directly, "My husband died a few years ago." Again, the focus was on *him*. No matter what, I couldn't properly own my new identity. Instead, I deflected attention from myself, softened a harsh reality, and ran from my pain and anger.

When my husband died, I was, indeed, in a great deal of pain and very angry. *How could he leave me like this?* Married friends supported me during my bereavement, often with fear in their eyes. Two told me that they had purchased additional life insurance on their husbands as soon as they heard what had happened to Jerry. A few distanced themselves from me. They would offer coffee, lunch, an afternoon tea, and then never set a date. I understood. If we spent time together, my loss might caste a dark spell, widowhood by association, their worst fear realized. They were afraid *for* me and *of* me. No married woman wants to be a widow, so I didn't remind them by calling myself one. And I didn't remind myself. I hated being labeled, shelved, and forgotten. "Widow" could be a convenient dismissal. "Poor Roselee. She's a widow." *I'm still me*, I silently screamed, *just me without him. Not a whole new category.*

But the word applied to me, whether I embraced it or not. In my long evolution from married woman to woman alone, from mere survivor to solo thriver, I had skirted a central truth: that widowhood described my experience, and that it had meaning and dignity beyond its sad clichés. Widow can imply a perpetual state of mourning, but it can also mean resilience, strength, and wisdom. I did not grieve alone in my room with curtains drawn, wear black, or throw myself on a flaming pyre along with my husband. I marched through, dressed in my favorite reds and purples, went about my business, healed, and moved forward, carrying my dear husband with me, and in so doing, rebuilt myself and my life. There are many ways to be a widow.

In the beginning, I rejected the word, because I couldn't accept the reality that my husband was dead and was never coming back. Though I wrote about widowhood, I couldn't talk about it. Over time I learned how to lighten its overwhelming weight, to integrate this shadow self into my new identity. Widow might be the first thing someone said about me, but it wouldn't be the last. It was simply one descriptor among many: mother, writer, volunteer, friend, happy person. I was ready to support women living without their beloveds. I was willing to speak to them about my journey and to listen to theirs. I believed that by saying the word out loud and demystifying it, I could help others struggling through their own losses.

It had taken eight and a half years to be able to state boldly and unapologetically in print and in public, that my husband, Jerry, died, and that I belonged in a desired-by-no-one category, the widowed. I'd finally accepted this central description of who I was.

Now when I address a group of bereaved people, I introduce myself by saying, "My name is Roselee Blooston, and I'm a widow."

Writing Life

Why did embarking on a new chapter in my writing life feel like both a birth and a rebirth? Part of the answer was obvious: there was a lot of labor involved, a lot of figurative blood, and real sweat and tears. When I began writing, I was a child creating illustrated poetry books, which were a secondary outlet for my ever-present need to express myself. Those first efforts rhymed. Later, as a seventh grader, I turned to haiku and got my first accolades: an Honorable Mention in the national *Junior Scholastic* writing contest. But acting was my true love, and after college, frustrated with my university teaching job, and longing to be on stage, I wrote my first one-person play, *The Phrase in Air*, about my idol, Edna St. Vincent Millay. I found this so fulfilling that I went on to write four more solo vehicles, which garnered more attention, including national and international bookings, and a glowing review in *Variety*, not to mention the resolution of my fears about becoming a mother—dissected in *Mad Moms*—with the birth of my son. But none of those efforts resulted in a sustaining professional career. So, I let the theater go. I let that phase of my life die, mourned it, and moved on.

Hence, my rebirth—a partial revisiting of an earlier incarnation—I was still a writer, though no longer a playwright. This rebirth required greater loss than a disappointing acting career. When my husband died in 2008, I knew instantly that part of the way through my grief would be through writing. Sudden loss demanded my whole self, first to get through the surreal setting, and then to understand who I had been during my marriage, and who I would be after. There would be no place to hide, and no desire to do so. I needed to write to survive, and to rediscover my essential self through the process. I had been preparing for this all my writing life. I also knew that I would be a different person, an *After Jerry* version of myself, reborn as a woman alone, and as a memoirist.

I won't catalogue the blood, sweat, and tears here. *Dying in Dubai* did that. I will say that I believe all writing is a kind of reinvention, whether an immersion in a new genre or a means to a new life. I often don't know what I really think about a given subject or circumstance until I write about it. Writing is the most active and cogent form of thinking. Words on paper or on screen clarify my thoughts in a way that rumination—the endless circular spinning of the mind at 2 a.m.—cannot. Circumstance told me what form my writing had to take to tell the story of my loss and transformation. In memoir, I had to drop "characters" and be myself, the naked role I had in some sense been avoiding in my plays. I had to start over, completely. My first memoir was both the vehicle for and document of that trajectory.

Friends asked me during my years of working on the book, if writing helped. *Was it cathartic? Did it provide closure?* Yes and no. I would answer that if I had needed to write my story solely as therapy, I would have been done working on it by draft number three. The truth was, that from the outset, I knew *Dying in Dubai* was meant for readers, for strangers, and not for my eyes alone in a private journal. Even when I was writing draft one, in a workshop, I pictured my unknown future readers and spoke to them with every word.

From the moment when the box containing the Advance Review Copies of my first book—ARCs, as they are known in the industry—arrived, and the one mere seconds after, when I sliced through the packing tape and ripped open the cardboard top to behold two stacks of *the book,* all thoughts of the time it took to get here flew from my mind.

I stood alone, in my sunroom, staring down at the concrete manifestation of my long-awaited dream. The story of my grief and transformation that I had known from the outset could touch and help readers I would never meet, was now a reality, and I was both proud and stunned. For what felt like a long time, but may have been only a minute, I didn't move. I drank in the cover, which I had seen on my computer screen many times. Its smooth, velvety texture rendered it far superior to the flat image. Rarely is an imagined vision expressed so exactly. This was.

Gingerly, I lifted out a copy, careful not to bend the edges. I breathed out. I marveled at the size and heft, using my hand as a scale. Solid. I inhaled the "new book" smell of freshly cut pages. I turned it over and admired the way the front cover's sand and sky wrapped around to the back and how the blurbs, description, and my photo and bio all fit exactly as I had wished. Tentatively, at arm's length, I flipped through the pages, congratulating my early insistence on cream stock—so much softer and easier on the eye than white—but I did not read. I wanted to save that experience for the following week, or the week after that. My publisher didn't need final changes until the end of July. Plenty of time to get used to the idea, to the fact, to the *arti*fact of my labors stored in that box in my study. I had read thousands of books; next, I would read my own.

What did I think about the obstacles that littered my path, but ultimately did not deter me, foremost among them, a two-year agent search and the nine months spent with one whose interest turned out to be tentative? I had thought that having an agent was the golden ticket, which was why I spent so long trying to land one but learned instead that it was better to have no agent than a bad agent, who would take fifteen per cent of any contract, even one I initiated. Weeks before I fired mine, sure that I would have to take such a previously unthinkable step, I drew up a list of independent publishers I could approach without an agent. After a summer of re-grouping, I began again, on my own, and got an offer from the first publisher I applied to—a small, non-profit, university press. My goal had been to see the book published, not to self-publish. Years of solo performing, which sometimes involved self-producing, taught me that I needed the undeniable legitimacy of a curated process. The publisher said yes, they would be delighted to publish my memoir, and that was all the validation I needed. The agent had been a necessary obstacle, without which I would not have made my own opportunity.

I sat at my desk, an ARC next to my computer—the solid, handsome volume containing my life and my work. Performing had given me many euphoric moments, but life in the theater was all ephemera; by definition, it could not last. The book existed physically, on its own, without me, and it could exist long after me. A writer friend pointed out that our books could end up in a yard sale that our grandchildren might come across someday. He meant it as a wonder, a legacy, a gratifying prospect. I agreed. It was with joy and deep satisfaction, that finally, I held my book in my hand.

Many readers don't realize what goes into the editing of a book. *Dying in Dubai* had gone through numerous drafts—at least fourteen—some, which I edited myself, and some, which an outside editor reviewed.

The first editors to comment were developmental editors. Their job was to look broadly at character, plot, story arc, themes. Like novels, memoirs must satisfy in each of these categories. When I handed in my drafts, I was nervous about what these editors might say, but also eager to address their concerns. That didn't mean I always took their advice; not because they were necessarily wrong—usually they had valid points—but because it was my book, and I was the final editor. I needed to trust my gut when making a choice between their suggestions and my own sense of what had to be said or eliminated. I am very grateful for that process; it made the book better.

The other type of editor is a copyeditor. These essential professionals go over the writing word by word and line by line to find mistakes in spelling, grammar, punctuation, and sometimes in formatting, i.e. spaces between sentences and words. I hired a very competent woman to line edit the memoir before I turned it into my publisher, who would then layout the pages in book form. My small university press didn't have the staff to copyedit and recommended that my copyeditor and I follow the *Chicago Manual of Style* as a guide.

When I turned that draft into the publisher, I thought I was done. But no. What followed once I saw the layout were another four drafts of back and forth between me and the layout designer about spacing, font size and style, headers and footers, blank pages, and the bane of my existence: the Oxford comma. That's the comma before "and" in a series of three or more, that *AP* style avoids, saving space, and that *Chicago* embraces. I had been trained *not* to use it, but as soon as I chose, for design reasons, to add a comma before "and" in the cover subtitle— *a memoir of marriage, mourning,* and *the Middle East*—I had to go back through the entire manuscript to be consistent by adding countless Oxford commas, making only a few exceptions for reasons of spacing. I won't bore you with *em* dashes (—), ellipses or italics. Suffice it to say, the lists of corrections that I sent the designer were long and detailed.

Midway through this grueling process, I attended a reading by Mary Norris, famed copyeditor of *The New Yorker*, and author of *Between You & Me, Confessions of a Comma Queen*, at my favorite local bookstore, Oblong Books & Music in Rhinebeck, New York. During the Q & A, I asked if she and the copyeditor of her publisher, W.W. Norton, had had any disagreements about style choices. She said yes, but that they had worked them out. Then she volunteered that the hard cover version of the book had been "riddled with errors," and that the paperback version, which we were there to celebrate, still had two. I was shocked and dismayed. *If the most trusted copyeditor of the most polished magazine couldn't perfect her book, what hope was there for me?*

After the talk, I handed Ms. Norris my newly purchased copy of her book to sign, telling her that I was both heartened and horrified to hear of her experience, because I was about to have my own first book published.

She smiled and said, "No one is perfect. Just do the best you can." Then she gave me a tip. "Take a ruler, place it under each line so as not to let your eyes race ahead, and go through the manuscript that way at least once."

I thanked her, took her instruction as gospel—she had forty years of copyediting experience to my one—and employed the ruler method three times. Most recently, during my final pass, after going through the Advance Review Copy, making my last changes, and then receiving a final PDF from the publisher for me to sign off on, I discovered that not everything was in my control. Yes, they had made all the changes I asked for, but in so doing had triggered a bizarre software malfunction rendering the layout a mess! I had a morning-long panic attack, took a deep breath, texted my publisher to alert him about the problem, and awaited yet another PDF to review—draft number fifteen.

So, I ask only one thing of you, dear reader: *if you find an error in any of my books, remember that it puts me in good company.*

When a good friend and Vassar classmate offered to pitch an Author Talk for me at the Jacob Sears Memorial Library, her local Cape Cod branch, neither of us realized that its event coordinator was another Vassar '73 grad. They both did an incredible job publicizing the August event, which—with my publisher's blessing, since it was six weeks before my official launch date—included a reading and signing. There's nothing better than the power of old school ties!

That was only the first of the remarkable associations that manifested that evening. As I waited to begin my talk, I sat to the side of a podium—I didn't intend to use it since I preferred to move and because I'm so short, I would have looked like a literal "talking head" behind it—and overheard a mother and daughter talking. I had placed postcards about the book on each seat. The young woman picked up one, turned it over, and remarked,

"Mom, this is from my school!" I introduced myself, and asked if she attended Loyola University Maryland, home of Apprentice House Press, my publishing house. The answer, "Yes, I'm a senior there, but I'm here, because I had just spent two months in Dubai." Ah, synchronicity.

A few minutes later, I was surprised and delighted by the coordinator's introduction. She was incredibly thorough, going as far back as my one-person plays. When she mentioned *The Queen's in the Kitchen*, and my long-ago status as a professional look-alike for Elizabeth II, I improvised, raising my hand for the royal wave. The audience laughed and I was over my nerves before I'd spoken a word. Considering the subject matter of my memoir, I had been concerned that the talk would be too heavy. No worries. Between QE2 and the romance and fun of my bus stop wedding, there was plenty of levity. In any talk, especially one about an emotional subject, it's important to *make 'em laugh, make 'em cry*. I did both.

The tears weren't all sorrow; some were sweet. At the end of the talk, I read a Cape Cod scene featuring my Vassar friends and fellow drama majors, including one, who had given me her professional coaching advice gratis that very afternoon. Together, eight years earlier, we had visited the Monomoy Theatre in Chatham, where I had done two seasons of summer stock in the seventies, allowing me to revisit the "Before Jerry" me. Before the reading, I had given my classmates inscribed copies and told them not to look at *Part Two*. This was why. They didn't know they were *in* it. I had managed to hold myself together, when I spoke of losing my husband, but seeing my friends tear up while I read about our little jaunt, I almost lost it.

Afterwards, a woman approached the table where I was signing books, handed me her copy, and asked when I had performed at the Monomoy and in what shows. I told her, rattling off five or six plays. "I saw them all," she said, "and I remember you." I was moved and humbled. Actors and writers often don't know their impact. When a moment like that happens, it is a gift. In that instant, present and past merged. Now I could trust that, like my performances, my book would reach and touch strangers over time. The very point of writing it.

It was two weeks until my book launch and I felt tremendous anticipation about what would certainly be a defining moment in my life—very much like the two other days in my past when my public identity changed: my wedding day at the bus stop where Jerry and I met, when I became a wife, and the day, almost exactly three years later, when I gave birth to our son and became a mother. The launch on October first in our old home-town, Montclair, New Jersey, would mark the moment when my status as a writer transformed into that of *author*. Though I'd had stories, essays, and articles published in journals, magazines, and anthologies, as well as plays professionally produced—the theatrical equiv-alent of publication—the publication of my first memoir brought me to a new level of achievement. An author is a writer who has published a book, and with the pub-lication of *Dying in Dubai* I had fulfilled the definition.

I reminded myself how momentous and satisfying the launch event would be, as I ticked down my list of *To Dos*: check in with my publicist, contact libraries and bookstores to schedule more events, organize the receptions, plan my readings and remarks, test my signing pens, practice my signature (even though I'd been signing checks and contracts my entire adult life), and answer the all-important question, *What am I going to wear?* At least once a day, I had to stop and take a deep breath, lest I become the author version of Bridezilla. I told myself, *it will work out fine—you deserve it—now enjoy it.*

On a particularly trying day, when I wondered how I was going to get from here to there—I was so frazzled that I spelled my first name "Rosalie" in an email signature—I stumbled onto the website for Oblong Books & Music, where I would have a second launch five days after the first one. I had meant to hit another link, but rather than immediately switch sites, I found myself mesmerized by their home-page sliders of upcoming events: *Booker Prize finalist*, Emma Donoghue, *Oprah's Super Soul Sunday* fav, Elizabeth Lesser, *Bright Lights, Big City* legend, Jay McInerney, and *me*, Roselee Blooston. I had to watch the loop of their faces and names, before and after mine, three times before I could begin to absorb its import. I wasn't delusional. I knew my career existed on a far more modest plane than these heavyweights. But even so, each slider was the same size and style; in this simple, direct presentation, we were equals—peers—because we had something fundamental in common: we were all published authors promoting our new books. I let out a sigh and sat back nodding. It felt good.

Launch month had been a whirlwind of bookstore appearances, after-parties, interviews, reviews, and appreciations via email, phone, and old-fashioned note cards from family, friends, and strangers, and best of all, oceans of love. As wonderful as these experiences had been, there was one small public moment and one big private one that were most powerful for me, distilling their impact on both a macro and a micro scale.

After signing extra copies of *Dying in Dubai* for Oblong to sell post-event, I waited a few days to return to the store. When I did, I made a beeline for the memoir section. There it was, the most satisfying accomplishment of all: my book on a bookstore shelf, cover face out, adorned with a silver "autographed copy" seal, propped against a few more copies, with *Napoleon* to its right, Mindy Kaling on the left, Michael Maslin above, and *The Black Calhouns* below. Like the website loop, this reinforced a continuing theme: my manifest arrival in the company of other authors. The simple fact that my first book sat on the shelf of a bookstore made the achievement concrete. It was a macro moment because it was public. I saw it. I felt it. And I was grateful for it.

The micro (private) one was this: the day after my official book launch in Montclair, New Jersey to a sold-out SRO event with an audience reflecting our entire family history, as well as mine before Jerry—even a grad school friend showed up—I entered my Hudson Valley home, tired but satisfied, and noticed that the copy of

Dying in Dubai I had propped weeks before on a high shelf in my living room for all to see, face out, as in the bookstore, was on the floor. It had been standing on my shelf for weeks, as had a few other books I displayed similarly. They all stayed put. Books didn't fall off my shelves.

Nothing else in the room was amiss. I shrugged, stood the book on the shelf again, and went to my bedroom to unpack. About fifteen minutes later, I reentered the living room. *Dying in Dubai* was on the floor again. In the same place. This time, I noticed that the spot was a few feet from the bookshelf, as if it had been thrown.

I should say that I don't believe in ghosts. I don't talk to them, but I do believe that we are all made of energy that changes when we die yet doesn't leave completely; it circulates in another form.

I looked up, and said out loud, "Jerry? Okay, okay, I hear you." Then I picked up the book and placed it back on the shelf. It hasn't moved since.

I had the distinct though unverifiable feeling that the book fell the first time, while I was in our old hometown reading from it to our former community. Later, I wondered if my husband was sending me a specific message, that he was with me, although I had forgotten to go to his grave. Jerry was buried in Montclair. I had had every intention of paying my respects while I was in town, but by the time the event was over and my son and I had our brunch debrief at our favorite restaurant the next morning, I was spent. All I wanted to do was go home. And I did.

The skeptics among you might think that this line of thinking is a bit crazy. I agree, but I can't dismiss what happened. It was as real and as important as seeing my memoir on the bookstore shelf. Jerry's energy was out there, whether between the covers of my book or in my new home. My beloved husband was in the world. Still.

What did I discover about myself by going through the process of writing my memoir? By telling the story for others, I re-told it to myself, not only the story of the final years of my marriage and its aftermath, but also the entire history of our relationship from our love-at-first-sight bus stop meeting, to our fifteen-minutes-of-fame wedding there, to our deep commitment to our son and to each other, as well as our funny, eccentric games, all of it evidence of an undeniable, unbreakable bond. I had begun writing to understand my pain, to find a way through it, to make peace with lingering uncertainties, and to remember my husband's love for me despite his demons. What I found in the process was my capacity to love *him*. This was the message—love never dies—that I wanted readers to take from the book. By turning my story into art, I learned how resilient and creative I could be in tackling the biggest challenge I had faced. To do this, I demanded more of myself than in any of my previous projects, in which I had fictionalized my concerns, staying at a safe distance from them. The saying goes: *the truth shall set you free.* There is truth in fiction certainly, but for me, that truth was a dilution, a mask of sorts, a mask I no longer needed. Writing a memoir freed me.

In the following six years, I had three more books published. Each had been gestating for many years. It was as if I finally had the nerve and will to send my writing into the world. I spent my adulthood as a woman and as a writer seeking to know, and find my authentic voice, and with it, my authentic self. This creative act re-balanced me; it took me through mourning and beyond. The publication process for each subsequent book was similar and easier than for the first. I knew the ropes and had no illusions about my reach. I just wanted my work to find readers, any readers. The number didn't matter as much as the offering, because what I valued most about writing was the process itself, starting with a daunting messy first draft, which I frame for my students as "making the clay." Once the clay is made, the real work (and pleasure) begins—the shaping, the editing, and the rewriting, again and again. That's the part I like best. I have learned that being myself on paper was the point, and I was open to wherever that lesson would take me. Writing is a practice, an art, and a way of thinking and examining life that I intend to continue for the rest of mine.

Return to the Vineyard

It had been almost eleven years since I set foot on Martha's Vineyard in August 2007, an island that loomed large in our nuclear family's history. My husband, Jerry, and I, and our son, Oliver, loved the Vineyard, not only because it was our favorite and nearly annual vacation spot, but also because it held memories that distilled the essence of who we were at our best.

We didn't own a home there. Instead, we rented the same Katama house on quiet Gerts Way again and again. We claimed it as *ours*, along with the Flying Horses Carousel in Oak Bluffs, where Ollie once grabbed the brass ring on two consecutive rounds, the gingerbread homes of the Methodist campgrounds glowing with Japanese lanterns on Illumination Night, the calm swimmable waters of State Beach, and the rougher waves at South Beach. After that last visit, we planned to buy a home where we'd "retire," though I knew Jerry never would. At Christmas, I gave him a pillow embroidered with the island's attractions to keep the goal alive.

We had our rituals, mostly around food: dinner our first night at The Navigator on Edgartown's waterfront, ice cream at Mad Martha's, fudge at Murdicks, Mexican food at Zapotex, French at Le Grenier, brunch at the Black Dog Tavern, lobster dinners at Home Port in Menemsha, grilling fresh fish and shucking new corn on the Gerts deck. We went to concerts, saw MV native Carly Simon jam with her sisters, and thrilled to hear historian David McCullough, another longtime Vineyard resident, and a hero to my husband and son, hold forth at the Tabernacle. We kayaked, rented motorboats, and joined an afternoon sail.

We took four consecutive dogs along with us: two Springer Spaniels—a black and white named Deco Bauhaus, and a liver and white Ollie called Zeus—as well as our very own black dog, a Labrador named Edgartown, after where else? We called him Eddie. And then there was our yellow Lab, Tisbury—we loved those town names—and nicknamed her Tizzie. She was only a few weeks old that last summer.

Beyond their names, our dogs had a special connection to the island. Deco loved to catch frisbees on grass and sand, and to swim off hours on State Beach or in Lake Tashmoo during her final summer. Zeus preferred being ferried about in Jerry's kayak, like the dog god he was. Eddie loved to swim, so much so that we would attach a fifty-foot lead to his collar to keep him from crossing Nantucket Sound.

Tizzie, on the other hand, didn't like water. Perhaps she was just too young; she was only a few months old then. In 2016, she died of cancer, not even reaching age nine, a shock since Eddie had lived to almost fourteen. Other than our son, she was the last vital link to the small but solid family Jerry and I had created, his final living gift.

When Jerry died suddenly at age fifty-three, six months after the 2007 trip, I was fifty-five, and Ollie, twenty-one. We were a midlife couple, with many summers ahead together. Or so we thought. Two years later, imagining that I had conquered my grief and could attempt a return to our beloved island, Ollie and I were to join my brother, George, and his family there, which we had often done when Jerry was alive. I balked. George wasn't surprised. "It's too soon," he said. A year after that, he too, was gone.

I began to associate the Vineyard not with peaceful memories, but with haunted ones: an island full of ghosts, canine and human. The double whammy of losing Jerry and then George, both of whom seemed essential to the experience, put me off planning another visit. Even so, I obsessively perused real estate listings online for Vineyard houses. I needed to move from the home that Jerry and I had shared in Montclair, New Jersey, but had no idea where to go. I kept coming back to our dream of an island retirement, until one day I realized that "our" dream couldn't be mine. I was single now. The distance from family and friends was simply too far. I eventually joined a Hudson Valley lake community.

Ollie called it my "answer to the Vineyard." For a time, its water and natural beauty sufficed.

By 2017, fully healed but still ambivalent, I decided that if I couldn't return to Martha's Vineyard on the tenth year after my husband's death, I never would. In that case, I told myself, the island would live in my heart. A friend asked why returning was more difficult than the five years I had spent alone in Montclair, or than moving. My answer: "Because there we were only happy. I'm not sure I can face it alone." The shadow of a future not-to-be seemed too dark.

Sometimes though, after letting go, the relinquished comes back. Once I stopped pushing myself to return and made peace with the island as a beautiful but ever-more-distant memory, I suddenly and wholeheartedly wanted to make the trip. In early 2018, I rented a Katama house through VRBO, one close to but not *in* our old Gerts Way neighborhood; I rallied my sister-in-law Jeanne, her twins (my niece and nephew Isabel and Leo), Ollie, his girlfriend and another friend of his, as well as a college pal of mine to visit me during my two-week stay. I had to make sure I wouldn't be alone on the island.

I worried about the trip from the Hudson Valley and the ferry ride from Woods Hole. *What would making the whole trek by myself, landing on the island without my man, feel like?* I asked Ollie and Jeanne to consider coming that first weekend, so I wouldn't have to find out. But work and schedules conspired to prevent them from arriving when I did. So alone I would be.

The anticipation was worse than the reality. After an uneventful drive, I arrived in Woods Hole with two hours to spare. Once parked, I stared at the empty space in front of me, only water in view where the ticket office and snack area used to stand and noted the new building, sporting a swirling map design on its outside wall, near the line-up area. I eavesdropped on a man and woman standing beside the cars in front of mine; they were having a political discussion. The man admitted he hadn't voted in 2016 and was more engaged now. The woman despaired. I got it, but I didn't want to start my trip riled up. I'd become a cable news addict and had reached my limit. The next two weeks would help break the cycle. This was supposed to be a vacation, and what did I need a vacation from? Politics, of course.

The ferry was on an open-decked freighter, the kind Jerry used to complain about—he loved his amenities—not the one with food service and upper deck views. I didn't mind. I got out of my car, walked to the railing and watched as we steadily approached a vast piece of land in front of us that I didn't realize was Martha's Vineyard until we were ten minutes from shore.

In an SUV directly in front of my car, a yellow Labrador Retriever with Tizzie's pretty, soft brown eyes looked out its back window. Some labs have square handsome heads, but not Tizzie or this dog. They shared long, elegant faces, so similar they could have been twins. Stunned, I couldn't stop staring. It seemed like a sign.

A moment later, a young father carrying his toddler son approached the railing. The boy couldn't have been more than eighteen months old, Ollie's age on our first visit to the Vineyard. The boy had Ollie's round face, chubby cheeks, blue eyes and once sandy, wavy hair. He wore a baseball cap, Ollies' favorite childhood hat. I couldn't take my eyes off them—the father with his echoes of Jerry, and the son, who could have been Ollie's brother.

Either the dog by herself or the father/son alone would have meant something to me, signals that the past and the present had merged, but together and almost simultaneously, I took them as unmistakable confirmations of the timeless resonance of family life on the island and of my impeccable timing. I had been afraid that poignant memories would flood me. But those look-alike sightings filled me with wonder, not sadness. By the time I drove off the ferry and onto Vineyard Haven's familiar streets, I knew I was supposed to be there, then, and that somehow *everyone* was with me.

As I approached Katama on Edgartown Tisbury Road, a salty breeze wafted through my car window. With Jerry, I sat in the passenger seat on our vacations. I remembered the scenery, but didn't have the kind of road muscle-memory a driver carries. Now I would re-learn the island behind the wheel.

I nodded hello to twisting trees and shrubs, shingled Capes, and honeysuckle draped over fences. The rental house had a circular driveway of crushed stone, shaded by trees. I retrieved the key under the doormat, and entered, delighted to find a charming home with a high-ceilinged living room and comfortable bedrooms.

I spent the next day filing my refrigerator with basics from Stop & Shop—a madhouse on any summer Sunday—and from the quieter Morning Glory Farms, a ten-minute walk from the house. Then I took a longer walk around the neighborhood to ground myself, elated that I'd done it. I was back on the Vineyard.

The next day, a college friend, who had retired to the Cape, came over on the Hy-Line ferry from Hyannis. I met her at the Oak Bluffs dock and flashed back to Jerry meeting my boat after a day trip to her home in 2007. He had looked so happy to see me, though we'd been apart for a mere eight hours. Even after all our years together, he had missed me.

Ever ebullient, warm, and smart, my girlfriend was a tonic to be around. She hadn't visited MV in decades, so I wanted to show her as much as we could cram into a day and a half. We had lunch in Vineyard Haven, where I was dismayed to find that my favorite book-store, Bunch of Grapes, had vacated its original location, replaced by a clothing store. Jerry, Ollie, and I had spent many hours browsing its inviting shelves, always coming away with a pile of books. I crossed the street to the new location and asked the cashier what happened. The store had burned down on the Fourth of July in 2008, but she assured me that the new store had the same amount of inventory. I glanced around the space, missing the old one. Still, the shops and waterfront had maintained Vineyard Haven's informal coziness.

After lunch when we went back to the house, our phones started receiving alarming notifications about Trump's Helsinki news conference with Vladimir Putin.

We spent the rest of the day and evening venting, but still managed to swim on State Beach and to take in Edgartown's quintessential New England streets with their white clapboard houses trimmed in black, which my friend loved. Before her return ferry, we went to the Oak Bluffs campgrounds, where we posed in front of its multi-colored, whimsical houses. We topped off her stay with a dockside lobster roll at The Lobster Shack steps from the ferry, another old family ritual. We had managed to have fun despite the zeitgeist.

In the decade since last I visited, there had been changes on island: no more Zapotec, no more Navigator, no more Le Grenier—the French bistro in Vineyard Haven, where Jerry and I stole away for a date night. Nevertheless, the Vineyard had remained remarkably the same. The Black Dog Tavern was still there, the food as good as ever. The enterprise now had stores in every town. I did my souvenir shopping in their Vineyard Haven shop for T-shirts and dog treats for my neighbor's dog. Home Port in Menemsha still offered a classic lobster dinner, to which I treated my guests; it lived up to our memories. And Mad Martha's many ice cream flavors didn't disappoint. Ollie had a banana boat, dripping its contents down the street. I made sure to sample Murdick's fudge, chocoholic that I was, and found it as delectable as ever. The view of Aquinnah's red cliffs was still spectacular, though we would no longer run through the tall grasses down to the beach. *The Vineyard Gazette's* front page tick map warned of an even bigger problem than in 1992, when six-year-old Ollie got a bulls-eye bite on his leg, prompting two rounds of antibiotics.

Chilmark Chocolates continued to make the best candy on the island. While in line, I met a black Lab who put her head on my foot. The sensation of fur on toes thrusted me back into my lost life with Eddie and Tizzie. Jerry and I had intended to complete our Labrador trio with a Chocolate Lab named Chilmark—Chilly for short. Unfinished business.

I did, however, accomplish one task I'd vowed to do if I ever returned to the island: spread Eddie and Tizzie's ashes. Ollie and I drove to State Beach with two full zip-lock bags. We walked to the border of the dunes and distributed part of the contents, then to the water's edge, leaving just enough for a last stop at Gerts Way. We almost didn't recognize the house. Gone was the wooded front yard, which had protected the small Alpine style home from view. We had counted on the old trees to block us from anyone's sight, so we quickly poured the last remains on the dirt bordering the driveway and drove away. Mission accomplished.

The schedule of visitors I had created to prevent too much solitude succeeded better than expected. I had two days by myself at the beginning of the vacation, and two at the end before I went home. In between I ran a virtual B & B—friends and relatives coming and going—with barely enough time to change the sheets and wash the towels. It was fun—definitely not lonely— and tiring, which made those final two days particularly restorative. With the house to myself, I woke up when I pleased and planned a day of beaches and rest.

I began at South Beach, needing to inhale the salt air, listen to the waves roar, walk in the surf, and take in the Atlantic's power. The clouds and wind reminded me of waiting for Jerry on this very beach as a storm brewed. In his usual fearless/foolish fashion, he had kayaked from the Sound and was late. We knew Jerry was an expert ocean kayaker, but Ollie and I stood on the beach praying I wouldn't have to call the Coast Guard. Zeus tugged so hard at the leash that it twisted around my finger, and I got a hairline fracture. Then Jerry arrived, exhausted, soaked despite his wet suit, hauling his kayak up from shore, and loading it onto our station-wagon roof, while I tried to hold my tongue, but couldn't. "Please, never do that again!"

The clouds cleared. I went back to State Beach and swam and swam. I walked the public water line east, past the houses marked against trespassers, passing one heavily tattooed man collecting shells, and decided to follow suit. When I moved, my downsizing involved cutting every category of belonging in half, including my decades-old shell collection. I picked up a shell, then another, and another. Back home, I would place them in the small white porcelain pot covered in raised shells, its interior holding what was left of my now precious eighties, nineties, and two thousands collection.

My last night on the Vineyard, I thought about the wall of black and white photos in my hallway at home, most of them from our time on the island: toddler Ollie marching resolutely over the dunes; the four year old, shell to his ear, listening; the little boy running down the beach triumphantly thrusting his find in the air; the six–year–old on my brother's lap sitting on our dock, the one summer we spent on Lake Tashmoo; the eight–year–old clinging to Zeus on a wave-dashed rock at Gay Head Beach; the ten–year–old standing in the surf, chest out, next to his best friend, both proudly holding massive gobs of seaweed; Jerry and Eddie swimming together; and our final summer, preserved as our 2007 Christmas card, with its family portrait on Ollie's twenty-first birthday, and its photos of Eddie in front of an "Entering Edgartown" sign, and puppy Tizzie, bone-in-mouth, posed under "Entering Tisbury."

I believed old memories would sustain me. Now, I had created new ones, a joy I'm glad I didn't forgo. Shops and restaurants come and go, people too, but the sand and sky speak to an elemental truth: the Vineyard was home. Whether with my true love or without, Martha's Vineyard was part of who I was, am, and would be. Ollie was a grown man in a serious relationship. Our dreams had changed, but the Vineyard was still part of them and would continue to be.

Before bed on my last night, I picked up the large book about the making of *Jaws*, that the homeowners had placed on the living room coffee table. The movie was shot exclusively on Martha's Vineyard fifty years earlier. The island had celebrated the anniversary with an outdoor screening the week before I arrived. I had never seen the film; I'm a real chicken about scary movies. But browsing through the week-by-week saga of how the film was made, using the entire island that I knew and loved so well, and its casting of the island's inhabitants in roles large and small, I changed my mind. I resolved to finally see *Jaws*.

Before closing my eyes that night, I smiled at the irony: the best day had been the last one, all by myself.

The next morning, I locked the house, lined up for the ferry in Vineyard Haven, and took one final look at the harbor, and the soft Vineyard sky. My car drove on first and would be first off. A deep satisfaction washed over me.

The following month, in Rhinebeck's Upstate Theater, I braced myself for *Jaws* to begin, resolving to focus on the familiar settings to counter my squeamishness. During the screening, I jumped once, but the gruesome bloody limbs seemed quaint by today's standards. Spielberg built the tension masterfully and the John Williams score did its job. I loved that the shark was hardly seen, and laughed more than expected, in intentionally funny places, and at unintentional ones—Robert Shaw's unidentifiable accent. I found the story suspenseful, but not genuinely frightening. In short, I had a ball. My fears, both cinema-related and grief-induced, had evaporated. It took a long time to return to Martha's Vineyard, but having done so, I knew one thing for sure: the Vineyard was part of me and always would be.

Best Day

The happiest day of my life so far…that is how I've thought of my only child's wedding from the day it took place on November 9, 2019. To be honest, at first, I thought it was the happiest day of my life period. But that seemed to foreclose on future joy, thus, strategically, I added the "so far."

You may wonder why my own wedding, or the birth of my son were not the happiest day. *Why indeed.* Both of those life-changing events were happy certainly, but both were also shadowed—the first by my parents' boycott and the second by my mother's decision to turn off her phone the night I was in labor.

My wedding at the Manhattan bus stop where Jerry and I met, attention-getting though it was, had been marred by the absence of my disapproving parents. They dampened the celebration with a gloom that the international media coverage—Warhol's proverbial fifteen minutes of fame—almost overcame. Almost, but not quite.

Three years later, I gave birth to Oliver, two weeks early and only ten minutes before our third wedding anniversary. That afternoon, just before we went to the hospital, I called my mom, who was home in Maryland taking care of my father after minor surgery, and told her, "The baby's going to be born tonight." At midnight, Jerry tried calling her to give her the happy news, but the phone rang and rang.

Mother called the next morning. When I said we had tried to reach her with the news that her first grandchild had been born, she responded, "I turned off the phone. I need my sleep."

Shocked, I blurted, "What if something had gone wrong?"

"But it didn't."

Two abandonments, three years apart, and the reason why attending Ollie's own wedding, thirty-three years later, ranked first on my happiness scale. It gave me the unalloyed pleasure previously denied.

My son's wedding was a treat from beginning to end, everything a wedding is supposed to be. He and his bride were surrounded by family and friends; both are only children and wisely built a network of chosen brothers and sisters. And his wedding was fun. It took place on the Staten Island Ferry, a quirky choice that reflected who they were as individuals and as a couple, with a nod to my transit nuptials. There was laughter and cheers. The love and support were palpable.

The morning of the wedding, Ollie used my Brooklyn Heights hotel room to change, because Christina was getting ready in their apartment. (They wouldn't check into their room until that afternoon.) Though usually non-traditional, they wanted to preserve the expected separation of bride and groom before the ceremony. When he came down to the lobby in his Acne Studio suit—from the Swedish fashion company Christina worked for—a hip and classic plaid that fit him and their alternative wedding perfectly, I clapped. He looked splendid.

Along with my sister-in-law Jeanne and my niece and nephew Isabel and Leo, we took the ferry from a Brooklyn pier to Wall Street, then walked along the water to the Staten Island Ferry Terminal, passing the old one, that I only vaguely remembered. (Christina and her mom, Terri, would meet us there.) The new terminal was a vast, glass space. We went upstairs to find my brothers-in-law, Scott and Ross, and their wives, as well as Scott's teenage daughter, Sydney, waiting for us.

Christina's friends, Mary and Ben, acted as official wedding photographers, snapping pictures as every member of the wedding party—six for each side—arrived. Ollie handed out boutonnieres for his groomsmen, baseball cards chosen with their favorite teams in mind. When Christina arrived, sparkling in a white swing coat and white silk pants, carrying a striking bouquet of fall flowers, she gave her six theirs—vintage clip-on beer cans. With impeccable restraint, the couple had decided not to challenge the moms with something edgy and instead gave us conventional floral corsages.

The Staten Island Ferry was free and always busy. To avoid having to wrangle all eighty guests onto the ferry, Ollie and Christina choose to limit the attending group to a core thirty. (We would see the rest at the reception.) Once we navigated our way onto the boat, we went downstairs to the loading area, which that Saturday was mercifully empty, no cars in sight. A few ferry workers watched us with growing curiosity, as we assembled for pictures of the wedding party and family. That level of the ferry featured an open, unobstructed view of lower Manhattan chilled by a brisk breeze on this clear late fall day.

The skyline receded as Ollie's old friend, Danny, began the ceremony, timed to fit within the twenty-five-minute ride to Staten Island. Ollie and Christina read their vows. Though we couldn't hear much over the roar of the engines, it didn't matter. Just witnessing the elation on our children's faces was enough to move Terri and me to tears. Everyone whooped at the final ceremonial smashing of a beer can under foot in recognition of Ollie's Jewish roots. And it was done. My child and the love of his life were married.

During the ride back to Manhattan, everyone posed on the deck for "formal" photographs in groups of family, friends, and, of course, the happy couple. Their portrait, with the water and skyscrapers behind them, a seagull flying above, and their eyes cast upwards to a shared future that had only just begun, is now the framed focal point on my photo wall. A picture of the newlyweds, Terri, and me became my holiday card that year; it didn't say "Happy Holidays" or "Season's Greetings."

only one word—"Joy" —in gold cursive floating over our heads.

After the return trip, we had a few hours before the reception at Smack-Mellon, a Dumbo gallery. "Dumbo" stands for Down Under the Manhattan Bridge Overpass, and boy did this gallery deliver the area's cool vibes. When Ollie and Christina first showed me the space, on Mother's Day six months earlier, I thought, *how right for them*. The cavernous, high-ceilinged room had huge windows, out of which one could look up to the bridge. I knew that it would be dazzling lit up at night, and it was.

The setting also had familial resonance. My first apartment with Jerry was in Brooklyn Heights on the Promenade not far from Dumbo. Jerry loved the architecture and history of the area and passed that interest on to our son. His dad was on our minds, but we didn't talk about him.

Two months earlier, just as the RSVPs were coming in, Ollie called to ask if I wanted to bring someone to the wedding. The question stopped me. I hadn't thought about it. "No. Do you mean a date? Who would I bring?"

"A friend."

I reminded him that my best friend would be there with her family, many of our extended family, and Ollie's friends, who I had watched grow up. There would be plenty of people to talk to. And Terri would be there. Neither of us had partners. Christina's dad hadn't been part of her life since she was a baby, and he had died suddenly only a few months earlier. There would be no dads.

After we got off the phone, I realized that Ollie was probably thinking about the weddings that we had attended together, the ones where *he* had been my date, if you will. Now that would change, and he felt bad about it. My sensitive son was worried that I would be alone, but I was used to it, though his concern triggered in me wistfulness for the mother-son relationship we had had, which was about to shift. He couldn't be my go-to person; he was Christina's now. The frequency and character of our interactions would alter, though not the underlying love. If I had a living husband or a male companion the import of this shift would have been softened. Without them, it was stark.

The gallery room looked grand and homey all at once. Ollie and Christina's design concept was "urban living room." They had positioned their favorite New York books on art and architecture, as well as photographs of the city, on the substantial sills of the giant windows framing the bridge. Two very long banquet tables seating forty guests each spanned the length of the room, adorned with greenery, string lights, and votive candles.

During the cocktail hour, the scene was just as I had imagined. Ollie needn't have worried. There were plenty of people for me to talk with. Ollie's high school and college friends, whom I still thought of as boys though they were now clearly men, approached me one after another for a hug and to introduce their significant others. One thanked me for being there when he was growing up.

"You and Jerry were so non-judgmental, and your home was a safe place during a difficult time." Another told me how much Jerry and I had meant to his parents, a poignant moment, because his father had dementia. The wife of one of Ollie's closest friends sung Christina's praises—how great she was, creative and kind—and wondered aloud why I didn't have a new man in my life, warm and lively as I was. I smiled, thanked her, and brushed her musing aside. I wasn't lonely in the moment and that was all that mattered.

We sat and Ollie took the microphone to welcome us, thanking Terri and me first, "the two people without whom this day would actually be impossible." He went on, setting the scene.

> "Coming to Brooklyn as a teenager was a bona fide father-son tradition. We'd head out from Jersey in search of compelling photographic subjects.... I took a photo of the Brooklyn Bridge looking down Plymouth Street, right outside. I loved that photo. It meant something. I just didn't know what.... I know now why that picture's special nearly twenty years after the fact. Love can come from anywhere. You just have to be able to see it. ...That we're back here, slightly out of frame and newly married, with the most important people in both our lives is as moving as it is perfect. We love you all."

Ollie and Christina had carefully planned the order of toasts, alternating his side and hers. I would speak first. They had given no pre-instructions. They trusted me. I got up from my chair and took the microphone, "Can everyone hear me?"

The assembled nodded.

> "Hello everyone! I'm Roselee Blooston, Oliver's mom, and I'm thrilled to welcome friends and family, friends who *are* family, to this happiest of celebrations! In order to prepare for giving this toast, I reread all of Ollie's wedding speeches; he's been the toastmaster for a number of couples here today. As you may imagine, this was an intimidating task. As many of you know, Ollie is quite the wordsmith—a born writer—now a professional one. I marveled at the specificity of each toast, the way in which he brought to life, through wit and anecdote, the character of each bride and groom and his particular relationship with them. But the strongest impression I had from these collective speeches was Oliver's love *for* and loyalty *to* his longtime friends and their spouses. Now, at last, he has found his own true love in Christina.
>
> Growing up, Ollie had many passions: dinosaurs, Legos, baseball, history, bocce. Funny as he is, like many a comic mind, Ollie is a profoundly serious person. He's

a thinker, though not an ivory tower type, locked away with his books. Of course, he possesses many, but his energy moves outward, towards engagement and commitment. He knows what's most important in life. Hence the many deep and abiding friendships and family relationships evident today. His father and I used to worry about his being an only child. We needn't have; Ollie is one of the most passionately connected people you could find.

That gift for passionate connection was on full display when he met Christina. A month after their first date, he called me to say, "I'm seeing someone, and it's serious." Ollie chooses his words carefully. When I heard that one word—*serious*—I knew that this was it. He had found the love of his life. I always imagined that, given his passionate nature, when he fell in love, he would fall hard and fast. And so, he did. A couple of months later, he brought Christina up to the Hudson Valley to meet me. Before they walked through my front door, I saw Ollie take Christina's hand and the look between them. Their bond couldn't have been clearer. He'd found his person.

Before Christina, I used to ask my son if it bothered him, giving all those wedding toasts for friends who had found their matches. Ollie would say, "Mom, I'm not going to marry the wrong person just to get married." And he hasn't. Couples in love exude an air of inevitability. These two unique individuals fit, as if they had been together forever. Christina's special brand of warmth, her singular style, her intelligence, and quiet grace have—remarkably—softened Ollie's edges, without sacrificing his sharpness. And she made him a cat person too!

Earlier this afternoon, on the Staten Island Ferry, I flashed back to the transportation-themed union that made this one possible. As some of you know, Ollie's dad and I got married where we met, the bus stop at 82nd and Second Avenue in Manhattan. Today's variation on the theme resonated—I loved that it was Christina's idea—and it created a new family tradition. Ollie loves family traditions, which, who knows, may someday extend to helipad nuptials! It also reinforced a deeper truth: that marriage is motion. Married couples don't stand still. They move forward, into the future, together.

Thank you, Christina, for making my son so happy—like parents everywhere, that was what Jerry and I wanted most for our child—and thank you, Terri, for sharing your adorable daughter. Christina, Oliver, you are each other's home now. Marriage is the longest, most intimate conversation two people can have. May you never stop talking, sharing, listening, agreeing to disagree, and playing. I love you both with all my heart, and wish you abundant love, comfort, and joy. (*raising glass*) Everyone, to Christina and Oliver!"

The bride and groom were seated directly in front of me, looking down at the floor with heads touching. When I was done, after glasses clinked and the guests cheered, they stood, and I hugged them both. I was glad I had worn my reading glasses because they prevented me from seeing the guests' faces. If I had, I might have dissolved, because it appeared that everyone was crying by the end of my toast, though I'd made them laugh too.

The other toasts were also funny and moving. I especially appreciated Ollie's friend Sam referring to my son as "an absolute wild man in the seventeenth- and eighteenth-century mythological sense…not afraid to be himself." I took some credit for that independent streak.

After a Mexican-inspired dinner, Ollie and Christina danced, or rather swayed, to their song—The Kinks' "Strangers." I agreed with its sentiment: *they are not two, they are one.* I had told Ollie ahead of time that he would have to dance with me, like it or not. He obliged and said that my toast was "beautiful." Then he thanked me for not being "morbid."

"Of course," I said. The last thing I had wanted to do was dampen the proceedings by emphasizing those absent.

I love to dance. One song wasn't enough, so, I persuaded my nephew to give it a whirl. Leo sweetly complied. From the day I first saw him, lying in the hospital crib, I thought how much he looked like my father, his grandfather. Now, in his twenties, there were even stronger hints of his father, my dear brother, in his soft eyes and quiet demeanor—three beloved men in one.

For dessert, everyone was served mini-cakes and churros. The bride and groom cut a small cake of their own. And then the festivities were over, having come off without a hitch.

The next day, on the train ride home, I realized that by simply being there for my child, I had healed my own abiding hurt. Of course, my husband and I had close friends at our wedding, but only my brother was there as family. We didn't have the strong and wide net of community that Oliver and Christina had created to see them through life. When, much later, I mentioned this to my son, he said, "It's easier this way," acknowledging the hard and lonely road his parents had been on.

I understood fully, for the first time, what my parents had missed, and I felt sorry for them, long-gone though they were. My father and mother had missed the deep satisfaction of seeing their child radiant at the official beginning of her new life. I had learned something important, something that my parents hadn't known. When it came to a wedding or a birth, there were no do-overs. You couldn't experience such momentous events if you weren't present. The best day only happens if you show up.

On Longing and Old Men

It has been seventeen years. *How have I managed to live alone all this time?* Day by day, telling myself that someone would appear. Someone would walk up to me on the street, in an airport, waiting for the train, and enter my life. He would smile, hand me his card, and we would begin. Why did I continue to believe in that scenario? Perhaps because I met my late husband at a Manhattan bus stop, where we experienced love at first sight, I am now and forever a hopeless romantic.

There had been some moments on the road in keeping with the theme; I called them *transportation flirtation*: the guy at the auto repair shop who couldn't stop staring in the waiting area, telling me how beautiful my eyes were; the man at the airport restaurant who sat down at my table and proceeded to recite his life story; the courtly gentleman sitting next to me on the train who glanced with interest at my *New Yorker* and to whom I felt a palpable attraction. In my lame way, I didn't pick up on the signals they were giving off, except from train man. With him, I fought the urge to speak to him, because I was unsure of myself in my new status as a widow. Technically, I was available, but I didn't *feel* available. I still felt raw. Just like the inept girl I had been many years earlier, I didn't know what to do, so I did nothing.

Living in the Hudson Valley changed my perspective. At first, I had great hopes, but since every place I went, I traveled by car, the chances of meeting someone enroute were slim to none. I'd become more solitary, though I was more content than I had been in a decade. To meet people and to do some good, I joined the local chapter of the Rotary. I participated in a library book club and joined the gym for three-times-a-week workouts. I made new friends. I was happy and lonely. Romance, companionship, and men were missing pieces that nagged me whenever I attempted to put them aside.

Longing welled whenever a friend started a new relationship with someone she met online. I would tell her how happy I was for her, though I was jealous too. Longing permeated Saturday nights—the toughest night of the week—when I ate popcorn, watched a documentary, read the *New York Times,* and danced solo throughout my home to Motown or The Grateful Dead, pretending to be satisfied. I felt it when I ventured out alone on a weekend evening, determined to not let my single status keep me from the many cultural events in my new locale. I rediscovered how much I enjoyed classical concerts as

I sat among the many aging couples at Bard College's Fisher Center. When I returned home without someone with whom to "de-brief," as Jerry used to call our post-event discussions, I wondered if, like the tree falling in the forest, the concert had really happened. And as much as I loved seeing girlfriends, they couldn't replace the continuity of a regular male companion, someone who would be there every Saturday for whatever—even to stay home and do nothing—maybe especially for that. I longed for one go-to person.

There were also dark fears that would arise during a crisis. *Who will know what I'm going through?* When Tizzie, my eight-year-old yellow Lab, was sick with cancer, I would call my son and my best friend to discuss the grim prognosis and the endless caretaking, but neither of them lived close by, and my new friends, though kind people, weren't real intimates; we were in each other's lives, but somehow still on the periphery. In my morbid moments, I wondered, *If I dropped dead in my home, who would find me and when?* Even without a crisis, I was acutely aware that days could go by without my seeing anyone other than the clerk at the grocery store or the guy mowing my lawn.

My isolation became particularly clear during long holiday weekends. Presidents' Day, Memorial Day, the Fourth of July, Labor Day, Columbus Day stretched from their allotted four days into a perceived eight. Slow double-time. I made the best of these stretches—reading, writing, gardening—but by the third night, I would be jumping out of my skin. No amount of self-generated activity could substitute for consistent social interaction.

New Year's Eve was even more challenging, because it reminded me of my marriage's waning days. Our last New Year's Eve together, December 31, 2007, was a romantic evening at home, a final marker—though we didn't know it then—of our union, still strong, despite the serious strain my husband's long-distance career had visited on us. After a perfect round of lovemaking, shortly before midnight, Jerry said, "We've still got it." I nodded in agreement, satisfied, and after so much distance, relieved. That night haunts me.

For years I resisted online dating. The very thought that "everybody does it" put me off. Since when am I *everybody?* My high opinion of myself blocked me. The bigger impediment, though, was fear. I was scared to start something new. I was afraid to rock the hard-won stability that I'd achieved in the aftermath of Jerry's death. This fear reminded me a lot of the fear I felt in my twenties, when I was an aging virgin, caught between the rigid expectations of my old-fashioned parents and my surging arousal in the presence of men. I had been raised to sleep with only one man—the man I married—but at twenty-four, in love with a boy four years my junior, I tortured myself (and him) with a two-year game of *will she or won't she?* The emotional effect of this bind showed on my face in the worst case of cystic acne I'd ever had or seen. Years later, I discovered that cystic acne has a strong emotional component: repressed anger, under which lay sadness and terror, a toxic combo, playing itself out on my mottled, swollen face.

When I finally took the plunge with my young and very patient lover, I laughed—not at him, but at the absurdity of my road to acquiescence. *That's it. That's all I was afraid of? Ridiculous.* But it wasn't ridiculous. It was, like many fears left over from childhood, one that could only be unlearned by rejecting it in favor of actual experience.

In my sixties, I'd begun thinking of myself as a virgin widow. I hesitate to quote one of *The Real Housewives of New York*, but Carole Radziwill had a point: there is a kind of "widow virginity" that feels like starting over from girlhood innocence. She, however, was widowed in her early thirties; the reversion to adolescence seemed more absurd in my case. I worried that I had been alone too long, that I had gotten too good at independence. *Was this self-sufficiency the clever way I avoided addressing my deepest needs?* Wasn't I denying them just as I had as a terrified twenty-something virgin? Yes, and yes.

These musings led me to participate in an algorithmic process I didn't believe in. I was the person who hated Zoom and texting, who always preferred in-person contact. But I concluded that I had to at least *try* online dating, if only to know what I was dismissing. What was the worst thing that could happen? I would meet a bunch of wrong guys and still be alone. I wouldn't be worse off. *Or would I?* My best friend said she didn't want me to disrupt the peaceful existence I had created for myself, but I had begun to think it might be just a bit too peaceful. I needed a little excitement.

In the fall of 2015, I signed up on *Senior Match*, an appropriate dating site for my seventh decade—long after pheromones had evaporated, long after first love, second love, marriage to my one and only, and widowhood. I posted my profile:

> *I'm relentlessly creative, highly educated, serious with a sense of humor, poised, romantic and stable. I became a widow seven years ago and have rebuilt my life into something beyond my expectations. Although I do not want to marry again, I would welcome a long, loyal, and loving companionship. Ideally, I would like to meet a kind, witty, well-read college-educated man between the ages of 58 and 68.*

I hadn't dated since 1981, and at that time most encounters—even passionate ones—weren't begun by formal dating. In the seventies, we hung out, made out, hooked up, and moved on. We paid our own way. Mostly. In my limited experience, the formal dates I went on to the opera, dinner, drives in the guy's sports car—a Harvard man who never let me forget his Ivy League status—or in a limo, with a man my father's age who'd seen one of my performances, were outright failures in the romance department. The man in question was either too old, too dull, or too arrogant. I preferred to be led by immediate animal attraction, a looser, cheaper method that sometimes resulted in confusion and sometimes, in heartbreak. The only man with whom I combined instant attraction and formal courtship was my husband. We went on two "real" dates—a lunch and dinner on the same day—and he proposed after two weeks. Within a month we had moved in together. One thing I knew for sure: nothing like that would ever happen again.

Nor did I want it to. I'd waited a long time to put myself out there, because on a deep level, my marriage had satisfied me. It wasn't perfect—no marriage is—but it was real. I'd loved and been loved. But the writing life was an isolated one and the speaking engagements, teaching stints, and editing gigs didn't fill the void. I missed having one special person to check in with every day, even if we only saw each other on weekends. A daily chat, a weekend date. That's what I wanted. *Was it too much to ask?*

Within a week of signing up, I was getting interest from guys way outside the age range—seventies at least—and even more disconcerting, beyond the one-hundred-mile radius I had set, which included New York City, but not Georgia or Spain. Clearly, the site's algorithm didn't work. One model-good-looking man wrote overblown romantic messages but said he was out of the country, couldn't talk on the phone, or meet for months—all red flags. Anyone looking like he did wouldn't need to join a dating service, and I had my antennae up for guys who seemed to be targeting widows for money. I blocked him. By the end of that first week, I was done, though I hadn't met one man or even had a conversation. It felt like a total waste of time. I didn't really believe this method could work, and asked myself, *what do you want?* The answer had nothing to do with men. I wanted my memoir to be published. Days later, as if the universe had been listening, I got an offer from a university press. Suddenly, I was too busy to think of anything but my impending debut as an author.

Fast-forward a year and a half later: the book was out, and I was having a great time speaking about it to potential readers. But I still longed for romance. I had had a fantasy that my book tour would yield a relationship, since the book was about love, marriage, and commitment. I expected a man to appear at one of my talks, make eye contact, and invite me for coffee or a drink the next day. Didn't happen.

Attempt number two: I had thought, after Jerry's death, that the next time around I might end up with a Jewish guy instead. My Judaism was purely cultural, but I mused that someone equally non-religious yet familiar could be the right match. With that in mind, I went on *JDate*, tweaked the profile, and tried again. This time I signed up for a three-month package, but once again the filtering system failed. I got sent guys in their thirties and geezers in Florida. I told "Flirty Guy," age thirty-eight, that I could be his mother. He responded, "You might be older than me in age [*language red flag*] but a woman as attractive as you can date guys of whatever age she desires. Good luck to you." Flattering and absurd.

I spoke with an artist/engineer, who seemed alarmed by my call, thinking I was a bot. I assured him that I was real and reminded him that we had arranged to talk. When he settled down, he went into a long monologue about his romantic history, how hard the rejection was in the online scene. He asked me almost nothing about myself. Afterwards, I messaged him that I didn't feel we could continue in a one-sided conversation. He sent me an "I'm sorry," and asked for a second chance. I gave it to him. Then he went over-board in a cascade of messages, six in one day: writing what he must have intended as seductive notes about how "I was the one," how he'd combed my website and bought my book, how attracted he was to me—*he would touch my face if I were there*—that he respected me, and respected *my need for someone to dig into my underpants*, then alternating with how impossible a relationship would be with our past losses (his to divorce, mine to death), and how self-centered I was. He was direct. I'd give him that. It wasn't the lewd comment that stopped me, but the projection about my character and the relentless messaging, which seemed adjacent to stalking. I needed to shut this down. I wrote back that he didn't know me, we hadn't met, and that it was presumptuous to make any judgments, but that I was pretty sure I should have trusted my first instincts: we aren't a match, and we were not going to meet.

That man got to me. I didn't deal well with strange, needy people. His temperament was a non-starter. Yet the brief, intense exchange forced me to understand something I hadn't faced before. Though I did indeed have needs, I wasn't willing to have sex with just anyone; it had to be with someone I could trust.

Next was a promising man who couldn't bring himself to meet me in person, because he was too "overwhelmed."

Then there was the guy who wrote me a considerate, well-crafted message, including his condolences on my loss. I suggested that we speak. He gave me his number and a time to call. I was nervous, but the conversation flowed. We both had sons living in Astoria—what were the odds? —and agreed on politics and books. He said he wanted to read mine. But when I asked him what he did all day, now that he was retired, he answered, "Watch porn." I figured he was joking, so I let it pass. At the end of the conversation, we planned to meet after the new year. And I asked his last name; he knew mine from the book event photo I had posted.

As soon as we got off the phone, I googled him. There it was: he had been brought up on charges by a teachers' association—he was an administrator—for showing inappropriate material to a colleague. Porn. He had skipped his hearing, lost his license, and was forced to resign. His marriage broke up. In our conversation, he had alluded to "politics" having affected his early retirement. What I had thought was a joke answer to my inquiry about his activities was his means of checking my comfort level with his history.

I felt for the guy. He probably wasn't a bad person, just a man who had done a bad thing. But I couldn't take him on. I wrote a polite note: *I enjoyed speaking with you this afternoon. Unfortunately, I don't think we can go any further. I wish you all the best.* I'm sure he wasn't surprised by my response; he must have known that as soon as I had his full name, his history would appear.

I continued to contact men I found attractive, who seemed "possible," even though when I began this process, I had vowed that they had to approach me first. I got no responses. One month into *JDate*, with two months still to go, I cancelled my account.

Six months later, I joined *OKCupid*, highly recommended by one of my girlfriends. All I wanted for my sixty-fifth birthday was a boyfriend and a Medicare card. After a bunch of phone calls to vet possible candidates—*Where are you from? Where do you live now? Tell me about your career, your previous relationships. And lastly, given Covid, are you vaccinated?* —upbeat conversations, with lots of laughter, I agreed to meet three men.

One was visibly nervous, sweating profusely. He rambled on about his current and longtime female companion, who wouldn't have sex with him. He wanted to "go away for the weekend to *have fun*." After he said this for the second time, I told him that we'd have to know each other a lot better first. I wondered why he didn't simply hire a hooker.

The next man was sweet but we both knew there was zero chemistry.

The third, an architect, told me he thought I was "cute," and wanted me to rush right over after we got off the phone. I said that I had some work to do and put him off for a day or two. When we met, I told him about my life, and he answered my questions about his. I thought he seemed the most plausible companion so far and told him I'd be happy to see him again, perhaps for dinner. He stood up, saying that I certainly talked a lot. True, but so what? I was stung, and realized that he was looking for a quickie, not a relationship.

When I finally removed my profile from OKC, I was relieved and sad. Not since early widowhood had I confronted my aloneness so directly.

After each of these experiences I vowed to never participate in online dating again and busied myself with the publication of another book, but the pandemic brought my isolation into high relief. Suddenly, my Rotary meetings went to Zoom, as did my book group, and I gradually dropped out of both, finding the screen-only contact wholly unsatisfactory. My friends, old and new, hunkered down alone in their homes. No more trips to the gym.

During this period, while I was working on my third manuscript—a collection of short stories—an old friend, who knew us as newlyweds, emailed my website address to say that he'd read my memoir and how much it had moved him and how sorry he was that he'd been out of touch. I answered that there was no need to apologize, and I'd be delighted to speak with him. We had a long conversation filled with laughter and memories. He lived in Park Slope, where Jerry and I had our first marital apartment, and, after the call, sent me pictures of our old block.

For the next year, we texted about politics and family. I fantasized that something would come of it. He sent me links to his favorite music—mostly jazz—and I listened, delighted by the exchange. It would be so easy to be with someone who knew my past. There was no one I texted with this much, not girlfriends nor family, but given the pandemic restrictions and our history, I made an exception for him.

In the summer, I suggested that we meet in the middle, between his home and mine—Cold Spring perhaps—at an outdoor café, to be Covid-safe. He demurred. He'd had a health scare and didn't feel ready. I understood.

On New Year's Eve, nine months after he had first reached out, he texted me that he still wanted to get together and that he knew once we were both fully vaccinated, we'd see each other again. I sent him a picture of the lake outside my windows. "Hope you can visit to see it in person."

"Definitely," he wrote, and sent me a shot of his view of Prospect Park West.

By spring, we were both vaccinated, and I suggested that we set a date to meet. "I'll get back to you," he texted.

Then nothing.

It took me a year to get over it. At one point, I became so tormented that I wrote to him:

> When you contacted me in late June of 2020 with a heartfelt note, I was thrilled to reconnect. I've thought many times, you can't make old friends. Your email and our phone conversation were a happy surprise, and it was fun to text over the next eleven months about politics, humor, music, and family.
>
> But of course, texting cannot sustain a

friendship. Naturally, I wanted to see you in person, and I thought you were on the same page. At the very least, we would have had a pleasant afternoon.

I'm not a mind-reader. Perhaps you were anxious or overwhelmed by some kind of crisis. Perhaps I was just one more Covid distraction. Had you simply said/texted, "Sorry, I'm just not up to seeing you. I hope you understand," I would have been disappointed, but I would have accepted your limitations and been able to stay in touch within them. As it is, that's impossible.

In the face of your silence, I was at first flabbergasted, then hurt. How could I have misread you so completely? Now I understand that, despite your first warm message, you didn't feel any obligation to treat me with courtesy.

This was all so unnecessary.

Roselee

I didn't send the letter.

I still wondered how someone who professed to care about me and my family could ghost me and concluded that he was incapable of a healthy relationship, as he had been many years ago when Jerry and I nursed him through his difficult divorce. I remembered something else: when my husband was clinically depressed, I asked him where his friend was and why wasn't he there. "I haven't seen him in years. He dropped out of sight."

Then as now, an undeniable pattern. I should have known better than to hang my hopes on someone that unreliable.

By this time, I was approaching my sixty-nineth birthday and had decided to stop dying my hair. I had been doing so all through the pandemic because I thought that my old friend and I would meet, and vainly wanted to look as young as possible. After shelving the letter, I picked up the pieces of my wounded ego, added a swoosh of red to my now white hair—a reverse Bonnie Raitt—and decided to enter the online dating world again, this time using *Our Time*, a site for over-fifties. I tweaked my profile—removing the don't-want-to-marry caveat, though it was still true—and adding "active and happy" to my descriptors.

I was pleased to hear from quite a few men and culled the list to about twenty-five, whom I vetted by phone as I had done earlier, eliminating the men who were separated but not yet divorced—there were several—including a man who was still living with his wife "for financial reasons."

"So, you're looking for someone to move in with?" I asked, not willing to ignore the obvious.

He seemed taken aback at my directness. "My wife wrote my profile."

I thought, but didn't say, *so she's trying to get rid of you*. I told him that I didn't want to waste my time with someone who wasn't available, and to contact me if he was ever actually free.

"You sound like a nice woman. How about just coffee?"

"I am, but no, and I can assure you that other nice women will feel exactly as I do. Get your life in order first, then date. Good luck!"

The list narrowed down to eight, each of whom I agreed to meet for coffee or lunch. These men were more presentable than the *OKCupid* bunch, although two of them had on-going relationships with ex-wives—one lived in the same house, the other hadn't gotten over the break-up and slept with her on occasion. That guy lunged for a kiss as he walked me to my car; I gave him my cheek. Two had never been married. One wouldn't say where he landed politically. One wanted to move to Thailand together. Immediately. Another asked me to attend his brother's wedding, which would take place three days later. He was desperate. I let him down gently. "I don't think we know each other well enough to do that. Everyone there would assume our relationship was serious."

Most of them failed to ask me a single question about myself, even when I picked up on one of their cues by volunteering a personal detail. No volley. No back and forth. I couldn't help thinking that they were checking a box—woman—and I fit the bill as well as any other female. They didn't care who I was if I had the requisite body parts. Perhaps it was narcissism, or perhaps, mere social incompetence. They didn't know how to carry on a conversation.

A girlfriend who had a lot more experience with online dating than I did, said, "Guys our age who resort to these sites are mostly socially inept losers. Otherwise, they wouldn't need a dating app. Think how many women they can choose from!" I nodded. There were at least ten women for every one man in our age range. When I asked her, why then did she keep trying, she answered, "Hope springs eternal."

And last, there was the man who attended my one-person show. After the play, I met him in the lobby and was struck by his physical presence—broad shoulders, tall, and very handsome. We spoke on the phone a few days later, and when I asked how he was going to spend his Sunday, he said, "feeding the birds and watching Maria Bartiromo on *Fox News*." Then he mentioned a Dinesh DeSouza documentary. Uh oh. Conspiracy theorists and MAGA. Friends of mine said they would have cut it off then, but he had gone out of his way to come to my performance. The least I owed him was a lunch.

A week later, we ate at a quiet tavern across the Hudson River from my home. I didn't waste any time. We ordered and I asked if he was a Trump supporter. "I won't make you wear a red hat," he said. I smiled at the quip and said that wouldn't be possible in any case. He went on, "You know Trump did a lot for you that you probably don't realize."

I shook my head and told him that my husband had been a Republican, but had he lived, would have, I was certain, become a Never Trumper. "You won't be able to change my mind on this," I said.

Then he switched gears and told me that he had been a serious alcoholic and had been in recovery for twenty years. His drinking must have been quite severe because he started to tell me why he left the force—he'd been a police detective—then thought better of it, musing aloud, "Should I tell her this?"

I wondered, *had he been fired? Had he killed someone?* I said, "You don't have to tell me anything on a first date that you're not comfortable revealing."

He seemed relieved, and said he appreciated my sensitivity. It wasn't sensitivity. I didn't want to know.

Still, he had stunning light blue eyes, and said he'd take me to my favorite restaurant for dinner next time. "Let's see where this goes. If we're lucky we will fall in love and go skipping off into the sunset. I just want someone to miss me when I'm not there, sit on my lap, kiss me, and tell me so."

I nodded, not knowing what to say to such a bold cliché-ridden fantasy.

Then he said, "You don't need anyone, but you want someone." Perceptive. "I'm going to woo you." As soon as he made the declaration, I got a chill.

"We'll see," I said.

He was taken aback. "What do you mean? I know we're very different people, but we're getting along great."

I smiled and didn't say more.

He walked me to my car and kissed me on my forehead. On the way home, all I could think was, *I have to get out of this.* I was confused and a bit frightened. The attraction complicated what was otherwise straightforward incompatibility. Damn. *Why did a man I could imagine being with have to be a MAGA alcoholic?* I realized that the alcoholism was a bigger problem for me than the political persuasion, alarming as that was. I respected his long sobriety but realized that I couldn't go down that road again. Jerry drank, recovered, fell off the wagon, the whole cycle. And although my late husband had been "high functioning," I knew I couldn't go through any version of that story again. I would be waiting for the other shoe to drop. Life with an alcoholic, even one in recovery, was always only one day at a time, and I didn't have the emotional energy for that kind of vigilance. I needed someone more like me—someone who wasn't an addict.

I wrote him an email thanking him for the lunch and for coming to my show, which given how many other men had said they would attend, was a gesture above and beyond. I said that he was right—we were very different people—not just politically but in personality. I didn't think we could go any further and wished him well in finding "all the love you deserve."

Not long after I hit send, he called me. I didn't answer. There was nothing else to say. He called again an hour later and left a voicemail: "I just wanted to know how I could listen to the public radio interview for that Pennsylvania event you told me about." Again, I didn't answer. I had let him down gently. I didn't owe him more.

That evening, he emailed me the following (The caps are his):

"Tell your girlfriends that I was going to WOO YOU! I can be a good FRIEND. If you ever need anything, I'm here for you."

Then his tone shifted.

"You're right. We ARE very different people. I WOULD HAVE ANSWERED THE PHONE."

Whew. I had dodged the proverbial bullet. He was hurt, needy, and very angry. It wasn't as if we had had a relationship. We had one date and talked on the phone three times. Thank goodness I hadn't slept with him! He would have clung on for dear life. I admit though, that I do think about him from time to time—the dangerous, sexy man, wrong for me in every way, but compelling had I been a few decades younger. At seventy, I didn't have time or energy to waste on what could only end badly.

I didn't crave "experiences," as I had in my youth. I craved simple companionship—the hand on my back or in my own, the hug, the chatting about mundane concerns, the daily witnessing that only physical presence could provide. I believed that out of that physicality would come desire and romance, both of which I longed for.

The men I met through online dating weren't men I wanted to have an ongoing conversation with, and even when I did like a guy and hoped the man would want to see me again, he invariably did not. The reverse was also true: the guys who wanted a second date didn't appeal to me. These men and I weren't in sync. The entire process, from scanning profiles for a glimmer of possibility, to the expectant phone calls, to the hopeful meetings had become a huge project, to no avail.

I began to doubt that I had the patience at this stage of life to get to know a man intimately enough to trust him. In our twenties, we didn't have much history to summarize. We could tell our story to a prospective beau in twenty minutes, and he could do the same. It took about as long for us to digest that story and say yea or nay. Now, we both had long and convoluted histories—*baggage*. Though I'd processed mine through writing and long talks with friends, I was wary of doing anything that could disturb my hard-won stability. My best friend had been right. Relationships were work. Rebuilding after loss was work. Now, I wanted it easy. And it wasn't.

Discouraged, I vowed to be done with online dating. For good this time. My return to the stage, coupled as it was with a book launch and big seventieth birthday party had left me close to burn out. I'd done everything I had wanted to do with my sixties, but my eighth decade seemed like a huge inner shift. *What should I apply my energies to now?* I was proud of my accomplishments and the attention they brought, but it was one thing to be admired, and quite another to be loved. I couldn't imagine writing again, any more than I could imagine dating. So, I traveled with girlfriends, rested, and soothed myself binge-watching family dramas like *The Durrells in Corfu*—identifying with the resourceful widow moving her family to an exotic location to start over and fantasizing about finding my own version of the burly Greek who loved her—as well as spiky ones like *The Split*, where I could wallow from a distance in the vicissitudes of divorce. At least I hadn't gone through *that*.

During the rough week between Christmas and New Year's, my isolation got to me again. I had to try something different. A few years earlier, my daughter-in-law had suggested that I hire a matchmaker. I balked. I was afraid of spending thousands of dollars, coming up short, and resenting the wasted cash. Then, I heard a sponsorship commercial on my local NPR station for an affordable matchmaking service. I filed it away, until during my holiday week purgatory, the name popped up again. On December thirtieth I filled out the online form and hit send. I felt better immediately.

A few days later I had an interview with the match-maker who runs the service. I liked her. She and I had background in common—a Seven Sisters education, a non-religious Jewish heritage, and we were both in our seventies. I appreciated her direct sensible approach.

"It takes between three and five dates to determine chemistry," she said. "You have to give it time." It was one of the four Cs, she explained, the others being character, communication, and compatibility. Sounded reasonable to me.

She wanted to know what I had valued most in my marriage. "The long conversation," I said, "more than words, an on-going connection and interaction."

She asked what I thought was the most important quality in a person.

"Honesty," I said.

She said that most people got this wrong. "A person could be honest and mean. Kindness is what's most important." I thought how true and how astute.

After our talk, I filled out her questionnaire. Only "matches" would see my answers. She picked the matches, but I could say no to anyone. "Both of you will have to agree to meet," she said. "Stay positive. This can happen."

She sent me four matches, two of whom I contacted. Both said that they were dating someone and wished me well. Perhaps that was untrue. Perhaps they just weren't into me. But at least they were polite—a requirement to participate in her service.

Then she sent me an intriguing match with an accomplished artist, a widower, who was a few years beyond my desired age limit, but worth a coffee date. I sent the matchmaker a run-down afterwards: our easy rapport, how much we had in common, his hesitancy to start anything because he was getting over a bad relationship and had health issues, our plan to meet again, and his lovely gift of a coffee table book on his art. I told her that I'd emailed a thank you for the book and then heard nothing. I could only surmise that eighty-one might really be too old for romance, or even a new friendship.

I had left out one thing. During our conversation, he asked me if there was anything that I wish I had included in my online profile. I told him that I would have added one more adjective in answer to *How would your friends describe you?*

"What?" he asked.

"Independent."

He tilted his head. "I wouldn't have liked that," he said.

I had no come back, no snappy retort. I wish I had said, *you mean you want someone dependent.* Not until later did his response make sense. He was a man who came of age ten years before me, when women were less autonomous, and he had a large ego. He wanted someone who would look up to him and couldn't fathom that a woman could be both independent and reliably companionable. I should have included this defining moment in my note to the matchmaker, but it took me days to absorb its import.

The matchmaker answered that my feedback—even without the missing piece—was "very helpful" and "at least I had a nice time." She would continue looking for matches. But I couldn't avoid connecting the artist's version of ghosting with the texting fiasco involving my old friend. *Were these guys cowards, rude, or so lazy that they couldn't bother to politely tie things up?* It seemed that ill manners weren't just a young man's MO; old men could be jerks too.

Shortly afterwards, I had lunch with a girlfriend whose husband had died recently—no children, but a long and happy marriage of well-matched people. I hadn't told anyone about the matchmaker—not my family, nor even my friends who had seen me through my online dating experiences. I wasn't hiding it, but I didn't want to talk unless I found someone, or unless, a year later, I hadn't. While I went through this new process, I didn't want to drain my energy by having to tell a story with no discernable plot. I didn't want to second guess myself or complicate things by having to provide updates. This was private, until I had something concrete to tell. Then I would tell everyone.

But I realized that I needed to relieve the pressure of processing even the one first date, and this friend, who had known me since my naïve single days, was the best person to confide in. She listened with empathy, though I'm sure, given her still fresh grief, she felt far from taking such a step. We talked about our mothers—complicated, difficult women whose admonitions still had power over us, even though we were old, and in my case, older than my mother ever was. When I brought home my husband-to-be, Mother had said, "You don't need anyone." I thought it a strange remark, until my father made clear a couple days later her profound disapproval. She didn't *want* me to need anyone. I married Jerry, but during my years alone, I remembered her pronouncement as a curse. Lately, I'd become afraid it was also a prophesy; when the Trump guy nailed my need vs want quotient, it was who I'd become, evident to even the slightest acquaintance.

My friend and I talked about wanting someone to hold us, to be there for life's large and small moments. Referring to the matchmaker, she said, "I think it's a good thing."

"You don't think it's too late?"

"No. It's not." But given my obvious yearning, what else could she say?

We hashed out the challenge of taking on a relationship with an "old man." It was one thing to care for an aging partner with whom one had spent decades—something she had done with her much older husband—and quite another to bond in our seventies with the future foreshortened and sure to include illness and loss. The saying was that old men wanted "a nurse or a purse." I didn't intend to be either, though I was sure I could be a giving and loyal partner. *Where were the men who wanted an equal? Was I really up for this?* A Sondheim lyric ran through me, and I wondered, *if I'm alone, am I fully alive?*

Despite having been alone for so long, Eros still had sway over me. I had crushes on random men——a guy pulling up in his truck to fix something broken in my house; delivery men carrying packages; a friend of a friend who could converse; and a thirty-something restauranteur who flirted with me, passing me his card with the message *I deliver,* unaware of how old I was in my fully dyed auburn incarnation. Now, with a red swoosh topping my nearly white head, I attract attention. A young man collecting carts in the grocery store parking lot called out to me, "Pretty hair." He made my day. They each became part of a potent fantasy life, which held more desire and satisfaction than my real one. The brain was indeed the primary erogenous zone.

I had hoped to end this essay with a triumphant *I found him!* but that moment hasn't yet arrived. Solitude is my default setting. Companionship is elusive. I do, however, have love in my life. From men. As friends. And I have decided to stop discounting their value.

Two or three times a year I sit across the table from a writer I have known for decades at a homey restaurant halfway between his home in New Jersey and mine. We hug before we sit down. The pleasure we feel at seeing each other is palpable, the warmth and love real. We met in the early nineties when his son and mine became fast friends in Pre-K. His wife and I would consult on school-related concerns and kept the playdates going between our houses. He and Jerry traded quips. We all got along. When I founded my writers' non-profit, he joined, and our respect for each other's talents grew. He and his wife helped me through the loss of both my husband and my brother. These were kind and steady people. After I moved away, they visited, and then the lunches began. We understood both the joys and frustrations of the literary life and the ways in which it intersected with our families and the world. We understood each other as writers, as parents, as people. "How are you?" from either one of us would be met with an honest outpouring. We could easily spend three hours talking about everything: success, failure, love, aging, politics. Afterwards, I would feel filled up by the intimacy of being known. I treasure our friendship.

And there was the theater director who understood how my first artistic love, acting, had morphed into a new one. I would have never returned to playwriting, let alone set foot on stage again, were it not for his generosity and support. He's gone now and I miss him.

Third but not last, the best man at my wedding, who had lost the love of his life, who connected me to Jerry; this man and his partner were the first friends to whom I had been introduced. My son and I consider him family. He understands loss and is living his own "afterlife" with grace. He sends me emails about lunar and stellar sightings in the Hudson Valley, which fascinate him, blocked as his view is by city lights. He calls and we have easy talks. We see each other from time to time in the city or in my area.

Old men all. Fitting, since I'm an old woman. Just because these relationships didn't include romance or passion, didn't render them unimportant. On the contrary, loving friendships sustain me.

During my interview, the matchmaker had asked me what constituted a "good day" for me. The answer was clear. "A good day is one in which I have talked to one of my intimate friends or family, having a conversation that is filled with love, humor, and mutual support." Still true.

These days, I embrace my solitude. Within it, I live a rich life of the mind and have freedom that would be hard to trade. Longing comes and goes, but the satisfaction of following my impulses unimpeded would be difficult if not impossible to give up. Only if a gentleman comes along who could enhance my already good life would I consider embarking on a new relationship. A happy widow friend summed it up, "It's love, or it's nothing."

Every Valentine's Day since my husband's death I send cards to my girlfriends and family. I like celebrating love, even via a Hallmark holiday. This year, my brother's widow sent me two dozen pink and red tulips. It doesn't matter where love comes from or where it leads, love is still love. Knowing that—longing aside—will suffice.

Upkeep

Nora Ephron wrote an essay, "On Maintenance," in her collection, *I Feel Bad About My Neck*, that had a great deal of resonance for me. She had a lot to say in her inimitable, wry voice about caring for her hair, skin, nails, indeed, her whole body as the years accumulated. Ephron was in her sixties when she wrote the piece. Referring to the demands of keeping herself in shape she concluded, "By the time I reach my seventies, I'm sure it will take at least twice as long." She was consoled by the thought that by then, "I will at least have something to do."

I appreciated her light touch, since having reached her projected age, I've been thinking hard and rather more solemnly about what to maintain and how much time is worth the process, because time is more precious than ever. My musings in this vein go far beyond cosmetic upkeep.

Sure, I still get my hair done, though I no longer dye my whole head, only the wave that frames my widow's peak. I never liked getting manicures and pedicures and stopped completely during the pandemic. I don't expect to go back, ever. My mother, an artist, did her own nails, keeping her fingernails short, I assumed for cleanliness when she painted. In the summer, however, she did adorn her toenails in bright red polish to show off her sandaled feet. I do the same.

The pandemic also changed my exercise routine. I stopped going to the gym and created an at-home regimen of walking around my house on inclement days and on sunny ones around the lake road where I live. I lift weights and practice T'ai Chi Chih, a non-martial form of T'ai Chi, and a type of moving meditation. I began the daily practice the year before my husband died, and have, to my surprise, kept it up all these years later, because the benefits were so evident. Practitioners tout better physical balance, but for me, the improved emotional balance was key. A couple of years in, I felt rewired, in a good way. I plan to continue exercising regularly—though not to the point of breakage—Ephron's issue—for as long as my limbs permit.

Ephron recounted "threading" her eyebrows. I pluck. In recent years, I've added my chin and around my mouth. No waxing for me. She was right about shaving your legs: at this age, it's hardly needed at all.

The thornier issue involves internal maintenance, my insides rather than my outer layers. A few weeks ago, I had a conversation with my gynecologist about when

I could forgo a yearly mammogram. Unlike with pap smears, which can be suspended in one's sixties after three years of clear results, there aren't hard and fast guidelines for suspending mammograms. I don't have breast cancer in my family, so the doctor said that it was up to me to decide when to stop. I know that cancers can appear at any time in any body, family history or not, but I'm with Dr. Ezekiel Emanuel, a renowned oncologist, on this. In a controversial article in *The Atlantic*, written when he was in his sixties, he stated that after the age of seventy-five he would refuse all medical interventions and monitoring. Sounds sensible to me. He's not saying that he wants to die at seventy-five, simply that from what he has seen in the world of terminal treatment, he doesn't want to prolong life, if death is inevitable. I have an advanced directive that says as much. He believes in personal autonomy and so do I.

I will continue to have an annual physical, go to the dentist and eye doctor regularly, and do my yearly blood work for cholesterol and thyroid levels; it's non-invasive and I've been monitoring those my whole adult life. I do, however, have a much older cousin who doesn't take statins, despite very high cholesterol, and who doesn't have mammograms, because they are uncomfortable. She's old, but she's fine. Hearing her bluntly assert boundaries around medical maintenance made me think about drawing my own. Starting with colonoscopies.

I had my first colonoscopy at fifty-one and my second ten years later. Hated the prep both times and feared the general anesthesia, not to mention the possibility of a surgical slip. (I had been blessedly operation-free my entire life.) After the second one, I decided that it might well be my last. Seventy-five is the age limit for regular colonoscopies. I was seventy-two for the third ten-year appointment, slightly overdue, because what I really wanted was to call it quits. The entire procedure gave me enormous anxiety and I didn't want to put myself through it again. I relented when the non-invasive sample test, meant to avoid the invasive one, turned up positive.

My primary doctor called me, always a bad sign. "You'll need a colonoscopy," she said, then, anticipating my racing mind, "I've had dozens of people test positive. None of them ended up having cancer." I put down the phone and thought, *I could be the first.*

I scheduled the procedure and spent the next six weeks imagining every possible scenario, and telling myself that if the news was bad, I'd want palliative care only, no horrible treatment regimes. Like Dr. E, I want quality of life not quantity. Of course, I reserve the right to change my mind. In the face of a dire diagnosis, I might want every possible intervention, however onerous. But I doubt it.

As it turned out, my colon was clean except for one non-cancerous polyp. "See you in five years," my gastroenterologist said, citing standard-of-care guidelines. I weighed the odds. Polyps like mine turned up in fifty percent of colonoscopies; only ten percent of those became cancerous. In five years, I'd be seventy-seven. *Who knows what else might happen in the meantime?* I would table until then the decision whether to put myself through the procedure yet again. For now, I believe that I'm done.

The word "privilege" is overused these days, however, it's apt in this context: it's a privilege to grow old in good health. Too many don't get the chance. For me, so far, I am privileged.

There are other demanding pipes. I love my home, but it takes a lot of time, attention, and money to maintain, like any long-term relationship. You might say that I'm married to my house. Keeping it going is my number one priority, but I've started to pick and choose what forms of home maintenance are really necessary. *Do I have to check my A.C. units every year? My furnace? My gas fireplace? My heat pump? Can't I just wait until they break down and then fix them?* I've learned that despite the vigilance I exhibited when I first moved in, the very same well-cared for AC-furnace-pump would break down anyway. Why not just let things unfold? So that's what I've decided to do. I waited until shingles were curling and falling off the roof of my shed before I replaced it—ultimately, more satisfying than any preemptive action.

I've met a lot of people in my new area. These new acquaintanceships are fun and easy and don't require as much upkeep as bodies or buildings. All it takes to maintain them is courtesy and neighborliness. I can call a local girlfriend for a lunch or dinner and have someone companionable with whom to spend a few hours. I like walking along my lake road, seeing a neighbor working in his or her front yard, then engaging in a casual conversation about the weather, our little community, the state of the world, or all three. These serendipitous interactions fill me up.

At the start of the pandemic, I called every friend I knew, both in the Hudson Valley and elsewhere. (I called my married friends too, but I knew from experience that being alone during such a scary time was particularly challenging.) Some of them called me first, which I appreciated, but for the most part, I realized that if I didn't maintain our connection, it might evaporate, not because of rejection—we liked each other, no question—but because our ties were tenuous. We were in each other's outer orbits. Only family and old friends orbit in the inner circle. I'm happy to see my acquaintances whenever I can and appreciate how little effort it takes for those interactions to happen.

So, as I begin my eighth decade, I've jettisoned superfluous upkeep. No more dying a full head of hair, unnecessary medical procedures, annual furnace checks, or pressure to stay in touch with everyone in my address book. My white hair looks and feels great; it's softer, wavier, and healthier than ever. The heating system works, for the time being. I eat lots of fiber and continue to take my vitamin D and calcium supplements. My girlfriends call, text, or email. We see each other when schedules permit and that is plenty.

There's one form of maintenance, though, that I do enjoy: weeding. I clean my own home and find vacuuming and dusting to be a chore, but kneeling and grabbing stray green shoots, ripping out the strawberry vines at my door's edge, and pulling creeping grasses from between the bluestones on my patio feels satisfying, even though the errant sprouts grow back weekly. Maybe being outside makes this mindless job a pleasure. Maybe it's the mindlessness itself. When I put on my broad-brimmed sunhat and long-sleeved garden gloves, I leave behind whatever is nagging at me. I relax. I've come to think of editing as the writer's form of weeding. Trimming and shaping a first draft gives me a satisfaction similar to ridding my yard of unwanted growth. Probably why I also get a kick out of cleaning my closets.

Life is about more than maintenance. The "something to do" that Ephron mulled over can't simply amount to obligations on a checklist. If you find yourself asking, *"To what end?"* regarding a *To Do* list, you already know the answer: *none.* Regarding regular upkeep, the end rarely justifies the means, especially in old age. The time it takes to hold on might be better spent, because "the end" is coming no matter how many manicures you have. When the people I care about, whether new friends or old, show up, I'm ready for a glass of wine, a chat, a laugh. "Something to do" should be fun. It should be spontaneous, involving no upkeep at all. I trust that Nora would have agreed.

The Talk

Memorial weekend 2024. After a lovely couple of days with my son and daughter-in-law, we sat down around my patio table, overlooking a lake dotted with lily pads, amid pots of flowers, surrounded by blooming irises, clematis, and weigelia bushes dripping with bell blossoms, for *the talk*. Not about the birds and the bees, of course. A different talk. The end of life one.

They knew it was coming. I had mentioned over the winter, that I wanted to go over all things financial and medical once again. Eleven years earlier, when I put various legal mechanisms in place, Ollie was by my side in the estate attorney's office signing papers. He had been in his mid-twenties and his father's death, only a few years earlier, still stung. He didn't want to think about losing another parent.

Afterwards, we went to dinner. He said something like, "You've got a lot of living yet to do." True. I did and I do, but there was no getting around the march of time. Turning seventy hit me hard. Though I felt many years younger, I was now undeniably old, with much less time ahead of me than behind. So, I decided to reinforce the wishes I had put in place more than a decade ago by having a discussion, this time including Ollie's wife. Christina would be his support system in the event of my illness or death. She needed to hear everything, as did my son, especially now, while I'm still well.

Even though this wasn't our first talk on the subject, we both experienced a certain amount of dread at the prospect of another one. I know this because on Mother's Day at the end of a delightful brunch Ollie had arranged at Gage & Tollner—an historic Brooklyn restaurant that Jerry had helped promote in the eighties—when I mentioned that I wanted to have this talk the next time he and Christina came up to my house, Ollie blanched. He had thought, correctly, that it would be fun to revisit the renovated restaurant. Bringing up end of life matters was the opposite of fun. I didn't like thinking about it either, but more than one of my friends had serious health issues and I knew that I couldn't put off the discussion. For all our sakes.

Earlier that May, I had taken the documents out of my safe and gone over each page, as well as the hard copy files prominently displayed on my desk. I forced myself to reread all of it and took notes on what I wanted to say. I knew that I was doing the right thing, having a second talk, and I imagined repeating it every few years from now on, but I felt anxious. No one likes to talk about their own decline and death. I was no exception.

One page at a time, I went over the desk files with my son and daughter-in-law—an updated list of contacts for the attorney, financial advisor, accountant, bank and trust accounts, insurance numbers, doctors, friends and neighbors, as well as other basics information, i.e., the key to my safe, passwords, lists of contractors to maintain the house, obituary particulars (with the caveat that Ollie, also a writer, could surely compose one himself), my personal effects memorandum (clothing, jewelry, books, furniture distributed to family and friends as Ollie sees fit), paperwork confirming the double cemetery plot that I purchased when Jerry died.

"I want to be cremated," I told them. "But ashes can be buried there, and the stone marker has room for my name and dates." All very practical, all very final.

Then I took out a copy of my Health Care Proxy & Living Will. I had given Ollie his own copy when I first put it in place, but as I contemplated this sit-down, I had the strong impulse to read it aloud. "I want to be sure that you understand my wishes and hear them from my own voice," I said.

Ollie, stoic in demeanor, nodded, and took off his sunglasses, so we could look each other in the eyes.

I read from the document:

> "I declare that I have discussed with
> my agent and with my substitute agent
> [my best friend, Shari, who had offered
> to help Ollie if he needed to go over

end-of-life-decisions] my wishes regarding artificial nutrition and respiration, and it is my intention that my agent shall have authority to make all decisions concerning these measures as fully as I could if I were able to make such decisions. Without in any way intending to limit the authority of my agent…in a situation where there is no reasonable expectation of my recovery from extreme mental or physical disability, my agent shall have the right on my behalf to refuse artificial feeding of food so that I may be allowed to die and not be kept alive by medications, artificial means or heroic measures. In such circumstances, my agent shall also have the right on my behalf to refuse mechanical ventilation, cardiopulmonary resuscitation, antibiotics, antipsychotic medication, electric shock therapy, psychosurgery, dialysis, transplantation or blood transfusions, and to instruct that pain medication and sedatives be mercifully administered to me to alleviate suffering even though this may shorten my remaining life.

I wish to live out my last days at home, where it may be, rather than in a hospital if it does not jeopardize my chance for a conscious and meaningful life and does not impose an undue burden upon my family."

At some point during the reading, I saw Christina reach for Ollie's hand. She had tears in her eyes.

Then I took out the folder on my Long-Term Care Insurance and explained how it would defray costs for a time should I need home care, nursing home care, or rehabilitation.

And that was it.

Ollie nodded. "I have one question."

"Go ahead."

"If you are in a hospital bed and your sister shows up, do you want her let into the room?"

I shook my head. My sister and I had been estranged for more than a dozen years; neither of us desired reconciliation. "No. I only want people who love me or at least like me. She does neither." I didn't expect the upcoming family reunion to change that.

"Okay then." Ollie put his sunglasses on and moved around the table to hug me. Christina joined the embrace.

I felt full of love and the reassurance that they would be there for me and up to the task when the unwanted time came. I looked at my son's open handsome face. So much had happened in the past eleven years, both good and bad—his steady upward career trajectory, his marriage, the loss of his dear uncle Scott—that Oliver had fully matured. Earlier that weekend he had pointed out the expiration dates on my portable fire extinguishers. He was paying attention to details, protecting me, in much the same way I had protected him when he was a child. Clearly, he was ready for this responsibility. Our roles were beginning to reverse.

"You're a real man, and Christina is a real woman."
They smiled at each other. Then I said, "You know, I
hope to have many more good years." More smiles.

And with that, we went inside the house.

Reunions

Reunions carry expectations and assumptions, especially high school reunions. Going back to the scene of our adolescent struggles/flowering/confusion can be awkward. For me, the ritual was less about the inevitable comparison between myself and my classmates—how we'd changed physically, what we'd achieved professionally, what we'd been through personally—than it was about using the return as a mirror that would reflect both my young, unformed self and who I was now—a positive (I hoped) picture that would illuminate the story I told myself about myself. The comparisons were there too, of course, though they hit me on a more surface level, and since I had spent so little time at the Interlochen Arts Academy—for only my senior year—the school lived in my mind as somewhat unreal. *Did I really go all the way to Michigan at seventeen to study drama?* By graduation, I had barely settled in, and then it was over. I left and didn't go back. Until I did.

Fifty years later—fifty-two to be exact; my high school reunion had been postponed due to Covid—I returned to Interlochen. I had avoided all the previous reunions, because I reasoned that since I'd attended the boarding school so briefly, I wouldn't know anyone, which turned out to be true. But I realized during the almost three years of delayed planning for the fiftieth, that I very much wanted to return to the idyllic campus on a grand lake outside of Traverse City, Michigan where I had won a reprieve from the stifling conformity of my Maryland public high school. I needed to be there as a much older person who still carried that girl inside her, to acknowledge the difference between now and then, as well as the continuity.

Though I was fighting a miserable cold, which had morphed into a sinus infection via the two flights it took to reach Michigan, I met a lot of people and enjoyed walking my old haunts: the wooded paths to the practice cabins where on any given day one could hear flutes, oboes, and violins playing scales; the Kresge Auditorium with its indoor/outdoor ambience overlooking Green Lake; the cafeteria, smaller than I remembered, but serviceable. Though I barely recalled any of my classmates—the ones I did recall hadn't shown up—someone remembered me.

I was leaving the cafeteria, when a very tall man stopped me. "Blooston?"

"Yes." I didn't recognize him.

"Your brother's name is George, right, and he played the clarinet?"

My mouth dropped open. *Wait. What?* "Yes, that's right."

"I lived a few blocks from your family. George and I were in the junior high band in public school together."

"Wow. How did you know I was his sister?" I wasn't wearing my nametag.

"I saw your name on the reunion list." The list included the multiple classes sharing the reunion festivities. He wasn't in mine; like my brother, he was three years younger. "I've been looking for you," he continued. "You don't look all that different."

"Oh my. I'm not sure about that," I said, pointing to my red and white hair, "but I'm happy to meet you." Then before he could ask me about George, I told him that my brother had died in 2011. His face fell, and he gave me his condolences. We chatted and I thanked him for the most meaningful moment of the reunion weekend.

I went back to my room and texted my sister-in-law and my niece and nephew. They loved that their husband and father had been on this man's mind, despite so many years apart. This surprising connection, which predated high school, captured the essence of reunion. I'm not much for closure—I believe that life is messy and loose ends don't usually tie up—but this interaction provided some. Though my brother was gone, I was still his sister and would always be, recognizable even now to one who knew him long ago. To this man I was both old and young, woman and girl. More than the concerts, dinners, cocktail chatter, campus tours, and class photo ops that filled the weekend calendar, this moment was what I had, unwittingly, returned for—one satisfying link from the past to the present, rendering linear time circular, one unexpected encounter that would stay with me forever.

Nine months later, I attended another fiftieth class reunion, this one for the Vassar class of 1973. My post-graduation relationship with Vassar ran much deeper than mine with Interlochen. At Vassar I had come into my own and made lasting friendships. My three years there formed me in profound ways—as an actress, as a teacher—and the more distance I had, the more I valued the experience. Starting with the twenty-fifth reunion, I attended one every five years. Once I moved to the Hudson Valley, Vassar's home as well, the connection meant even more. I lived close enough to regularly attend campus lectures and performances. College had anchored my young adulthood, and now it anchored my senior years. I spent weeks getting ready for the fiftieth college reunion. I would host four classmates—fellow drama majors—and transformed my house into a sort of bed and breakfast. (We'd have the rest of our meals on campus.)

The first evening, the gals and I travelled from my home in Northern Dutchess County, to the Vassar campus in Southern Dutchess. As we walked across the quad of dormitories to the hall where the class dinner would take place, we must have been beaming, because a photographer, a woman hired to record every aspect of the reunion festivities, asked if she could take our picture. We were all dressed to the nines—I in a sleek silvery sheath from my favorite Rhinebeck dress shop. "Sure," we said.

We stopped by the dorm designated for our class and picked up our ID lanyards. On the way out, another photographer, a cute guy with salt and pepper hair, asked if he could take our photo with the class banner. Of course. We relished the attention.

He and I exchanged glances. "I like your energy," he said. *Was he flirting with me?* I thanked him, excited. The knowledge and confidence I had earned over the years must have given me a glow that, despite my lack of pheromones, attracted him. Happiness was attractive, and I was very happy that evening.

At the dinner, I meandered through the room and found my freshman roommate, who I'd last seen at our fortieth reunion. She was as beautiful as ever with her soulful Giotto-esque face and serious intelligent eyes, and as kind. She became an attorney and financial planner and had seen me through the first phase of organizing my life as a widow. We chatted and planned to meet for the class lunch the next day.

Since 1973 was the last all-female class at Vassar, there were few men at our reunion—mostly spouses of the women. (I had entered with the first coed class, the class of 1974, which didn't have many men either, then graduated in three years, hence my seventy-three designation.) The drama majors gathered around one table; at the far end stood a slim man with white hair. R? I knew he was coming, because I had coordinated the drama crowd. He had emailed me to look for a white-haired guy. I had answered back, "Me, too. With a red streak."

He looked at me, and I at him. Then he came over, picked me up off the ground, and swung me around. When he put me down, he said, "You look exactly the same."

"Except for the hair." I smiled.

He, however, looked entirely different. R was no longer the shy young film major with the bushy head, but a well-groomed man of seventy-one. We chatted during dinner, and I found out that he was divorced, with one grown daughter, to whom he was close.

"How does it feel to be a successful author?" he asked.

I wanted to correct him. *No money, no success.* But I didn't. It was true that my writing life had been more successful than my acting life. "Good," I answered, "but you're the one among us who's a real success." He was a producer in California.

"That's because I wasn't an actor. That life is so much more difficult." A kind response.

When the reunion committee chair introduced its members and butchered my last name—saying "Bloostein" instead of "Blooston," he and I exchanged glances. "My name gets mangled all the time too," he said. We're both Jewish. Significant, I thought, and preferable to *JDate*. We had history.

As the evening wound down, I gave him my card, and said how great it had been to see him. He wasn't going to the class parade the next day or the drama dinner the next evening, a mix-up he apologized for. I didn't expect to see him again.

Since ours was the honored class—a tradition for the fiftieth reunion class—we were accompanied on our parade by a brass band playing seventies favorites. I danced the entire route, buoyed by onlookers of all ages clapping and hooting their approval. I love to dance, and do so solo every Saturday night, bounding around my house to whatever my public radio station happened to be playing. I learned when my husband was away in Dubai that I could banish the weekend blues—the time I missed him most—by dancing, a practice that has been validated by psychological studies. For me it was intuitive. I danced through both mourning and my move to a new home and a new life. Dancing became a habit. No matter what kind of day I'd had, I couldn't be anxious or sad or lonely if I was dancing. I hadn't planned to dance during the class parade. I simply responded to the music as I would have alone at home. I wasn't performing, but rather expressing the jubilation I felt. Fifty years earlier, I would not have been this spontaneous. Now, I was free to stomp to the beat, and free at this landmark moment to demonstrate my euphoria for all to see.

Who should be on the sidelines, but the photographers? The young woman, who captured me and my friends the evening before, waved and took a shot. At the end of the route, the band played "Jeremiah Was a Bullfrog," and the rest of our class followed my lead and boogied too.

Flirty Photographer knelt on the ground, snapping away. "I'd love to dance with you, but my job is to take your picture." He saw me and liked what he saw.

At lunch in the science building's glass lobby, which hadn't been around in the seventies, I sat next to my roommate. We caught up about our grown children, her life in Florida and Australia—her husband's home country—and vowed to stay in closer touch. The college president made the rounds of the tables, and when I told her that we had been freshman roommates, she offered to take our picture.

A few hours later, after I sold all the books that I'd brought to the Alumni Authors Meet and Greet at the college bookstore, I went to a reception for donors on the lawn in front of the library. It was under a huge tent, and there must have been three hundred people milling around. I didn't see anyone I knew, so I made my way to the hors d'oeuvres table.

"Roselee Blooston." I turned and there was R, beaming.

"Oh, hi. I didn't think you'd be here," I said. We chatted. I told him about the book sales and the parade dancing. He and another classmate he was staying with had gone hiking on a trail my husband used to frequent.

"Sorry I missed it," he said, referring to my dancing moment, and told me that he comes east for work a few times a year.

"Send me your phone number so we can keep in touch. I'd be happy to come down to the city on the train for lunch or a museum," I said. Knowing that he wouldn't be at the drama dinner that evening, I told him how glad I was to see him again. Then I reached up and touched his cheek. He blushed. I didn't, but my boldness surprised both of us. Another spontaneous act I wouldn't have dared five decades earlier. We parted and spent the rest of the reception across the tent from each other.

Elated, I floated to the drama dinner at an Italian restaurant one block from campus. We sat outside under an awning, dodging a light rain. We giggled as I told my girlfriends about my encounter with R. We were twenty again. As we stood to leave, I felt a tap on my shoulder. It was Flirty Photographer.

My friends shot me knowing looks. "We'll meet you at the car," they said, and scattered.

He wanted to share the photos he'd taken of me dancing. "Send them to me," I said, holding up my phone. He told me that he split his time between Poughkeepsie, New York and Florida. "Text me if you'd like to have coffee," I suggested. He was fiftyish, and I could have been his mother, but I recognized chemistry's zing.

"Will do," he said. We hugged goodbye.

On the car ride home, my friends and I laughed hysterically at my boy-crazy day. Two of them lived in Florida each winter. "Find out where exactly he lives." I was laughing so hard that I could barely move my fingers to type the question.

A few moments later, he texted the location, a couple of hours north of my friends. Everyone shrieked. We seemed to be reverting further—not to twenty, but to fifteen.

The next morning, the last of our weekend together, I awoke to a six-a.m. email from R with his contact information and a wish that we "stay in touch." I knocked on my friend's door—my bedroom, since I was sleeping on the living room couch—and breathlessly shared his missive. We made much of the email's time stamp. "He was thinking of you all night," my friend said. Now we were thirteen. Suddenly, I was afraid to make a wrong move, and she coached me on what to say in response.

After everyone left, I was exhausted, but also recharged with the hope that maybe now—past my "sell by" date—I would get another chance at love. I felt like a girl again, but now a girl confident in her power and delighted to exert it. No matter what happened next, it had been a magical two days.

For the rest of the summer, I waited to see if R would engage with me. He didn't. A disappointment and a reality check. We lived on opposite coasts, and I had no idea if he was already in a relationship.

In the early fall, *The Vassar Quarterly*, our alumni magazine, arrived in my mailbox. I thumbed through and smiled at the section about reunion weekend. *I should cut this out and save it*, I thought, as I looked at the photo of our pink and grey class of seventy-three banner. Then I turned the page and gasped.

On the top of the next page, in the right-hand quarter, was a close-up of me, arms in the air, grinning like crazy, dancing. Of all the thousands of photos that were taken that day, mine had been chosen to epitomize the sheer joy of the reunion. I must say that the red-orange streak in my gray-white hair and the complementary outfit—a gray and red dress and fiery cardigan, which I had carefully chosen—looked just right. A stylist couldn't have done better. The use of this image, which captured me at my happiest, turned out to be a greater validation than applause for a performance or an award for a book. It meant that I, not my work, not my effort, but I alone, simply rejoicing in the moment, was enough. At seventy, I had indeed, arrived. And to top it off, the unexpected sparks with the opposite sex had rejuvenated me. Both old and young, I was whole, finally, and it showed.

I texted my Vassar friends to find out if they'd seen the picture. "Dancing Queen," one responded.

R thought it was a "hoot," and sent me a large digital copy.

I texted Flirty Photographer—it was his shot after all—and he seemed glad to know that it had stood out. "Keep dancing," he said. The same thing my son had told me when I slipped into over-thinking about when or whether to reach out to R.

"I will."

And I have.

Family reunions have a different atmosphere than school ones. They are personal events, layered with generations of history, which, depending on whose perspective dominates, could either reinforce the stories we told ourselves about who we were or clash with them. This may be why there had been few such gatherings for my marital family and none for my family of origin.

My parents, my brother, sister, and I formed a nuclear bond that for several years expanded to include my Isaacs uncles—my mother's brothers—their wives, and their children, my cousins. (My father had no close living relatives.) We lived far from each other, so we rarely got together, but I remember each of my uncles distinctly: the oldest, Aurel—his full name, Marcus Aurelius—who was twenty-one years older than my mother, a big barrel of a man with a warm laugh; Reg, an erudite Harvard professor; Charlie, a successful Hollywood comedy writer, as funny as his profession would indicate; Alvin, an intrepid world traveler, who brought my mother an international collection of miniature shoes, which I still display in a bedroom cabinet; and Kenny, an astute psychologist, who lived to be one hundred and one.

My mother, Leone, was the youngest and when her mother died, she returned to Minneapolis. Grandmother Sophia had appointed her the household executor, but when Mother walked through the home, she found some of her brothers had already taken whatever they wanted. She came home to us with only a Russian samovar, which now sits in the center of my living area on a curved hunt table my husband and I had found in an Atlantic Avenue antique shop when we lived in Brooklyn. I will never forget the shock, hurt, and anger on Mother's face when we picked her up at the airport afterwards. She cut off contact with her siblings until her final illness three decades later—too late for real reconciliation, as Uncle Kenny bemoaned to me long after her death. I learned the other side from my uncles, that they had supported Mother and Grandmother for many years and felt entitled to some mementos. My mother felt that their actions showed disrespect for her and for their mother's last wishes; she would have given them what they wanted, if only they'd asked first. She had a point.

This break with her family meant that my brother, sister, and I were deprived of ongoing relationships with our many cousins—a lack I felt viscerally. I missed them, though I didn't really know them. It wasn't until adulthood that we made efforts to meet and reclaim our connection. But though the warmth between us was real, it didn't *take*, not like it would have if we'd established an organic back and forth through childhood play or if we'd hung out as teenagers. It was as if we were trying to learn a new language as adults. The young learn new tongues and create familial bonds with ease. Adults don't.

The exception: D and M, my two oldest cousins. D, the eldest, was in her mid-eighties, and still worked as a journalist. After Jerry died, she and I had many conversations. She had been through her own wrenching losses, and she had wisdom to impart. Her kind and no-nonsense nature buoyed me up. And she was one of those women who looked eternally young; her spritely, elfin demeanor never faded.

My second oldest cousin, M, was an extremely accomplished professor, author, cabaret singer, and gourmet cook, who exhibited more energy than anyone I knew. When she was eighteen or so, she stayed with my family one summer while she studied at The Corcoran School of Art. My mother expected her to watch over me and my brother and sister in her free time. I remember thinking how sophisticated she was with her bohemian skirts and peasant blouses. (I was seven.) Now we were all old ladies. Neither the eleven years between M and me nor the thirteen between D and me mattered a whit. We were peers.

The three of us decided to have our own mini reunion in New York City. D and I worried that we wouldn't be able to keep up with our on-the-go cousin, but somehow, we managed. For once, I felt like the little sister, not the eldest, as I was in my family of origin. And because neither of my cousins had sisters, they told me that they felt the same.

We packed in a lot: museum-going to the Metropolitan Museum of Art and the Museum of Modern Art, a trip to the Ground Zero memorial, and a long walk from the High Line to our hotel in lower Manhattan—a dubious decision on such a hot August day, but we made it— as well as fine dining. M, expert that she was, picked the restaurants, including a superb Japanese establishment. My son met us for a meal in Chinatown. Though Ollie knew D well—she had been there for him during his time at the University of Chicago and her husband took him to Cubs games—he had never met M. This was what I wanted: to reclaim relations that had been taken for granted before it was too late.

The best part of spending time with my cousins was hearing stories about the grandmother they knew intimately, whom I did not. D was partly raised by our grandmother and M would spend summers with them. They both said that Grandmother had a beautiful singing voice and had made sure M got singing lessons, and that though Grandmother didn't have much money, she dressed beautifully, in custom-made suits and dresses. I recognized this as the origin of my mother's (and my) strong fashion sense.

That summer weekend in New York had been worth waiting for. Being with my cousins was a true tonic for years of family detachment. We could talk about what our parents had been through—the misunderstandings and hard feelings—and make sense of it together. We decided to make our trio reunions an annual event. The next summer we met in Chicago and again had a blast. We stayed at the legendary Palmer House and took in the Chicago Art Institute, Millennium Park, two plays, (one at the famed Steppenwolf Theatre) and ate extraordinary meals at restaurants M chose with impeccable discernment.

It was during this second weekend that we hatched a plan to bring the rest of the cousins, and their children, now grown—our second cousins—together for a larger family reunion. D felt strongly that the reunion should take place in Minneapolis, where Grandmother had raised her family. She wanted the younger family members to meet each other, so that the relationships could continue after we, the elders, were gone. We decided to first send out an email to learn if our relatives wanted to be on a family mailing list. Most did. Then we floated the idea of a summer family reunion in Minnesota. Again, most of the extended family agreed.

The first person to respond to our email, minutes after it went out, was my sister. She RSVP'd, "Yes. Sounds fun." Of course, I knew that she was on the list and had talked over the situation with my cousins. My sister and I had been estranged for years. I thought of our rupture as a divorce and not an amicable one. I had no desire to reconnect with her, but I felt that it wouldn't be fair or proper to exclude her from this family reunion just because she and I weren't speaking. There would be plenty of other people to talk to. Still, when she jumped at the offer, I was rattled. I wanted to run.

D sensed my discomfort and suggested that it wasn't too late to cancel the whole thing, that we could beg off for health or work reasons. "We could always do it next year," she said.

The seed for this event had taken root in me years earlier. I had helped engineer this big family reunion; I just didn't want the smaller more fraught one. But I couldn't back out. "No, it's now or never," I said, committing as the words left my mouth.

Before the Minneapolis event took place, I attended yet another reunion, this one with the family I had married into. In June 2023, fifteen of us, including my son and daughter-in-law, met at the historic nineteenth century Wyalusing Hotel in Bradford County, Pennsylvania for a laid-back weekend of stories and simple meals. I hadn't seen my grown nieces and nephew for decades; we lived so far-afield. It would be the first time I would meet my nephew's wife and youngest child as well. I was glad to be there and had no agenda, other than being present.

It had been a hard year.

Ten months earlier, we had lost my brother-in-law Scott to pancreatic cancer. Only his sister Kathy, the oldest, and Ross, the baby of the family, were left. Ross and Scott had gone above and beyond when Jerry was stricken in Dubai, flying from their homes on the west coast to support me and Ollie. They continued to stand up for us throughout the following painful years and really stepped up for Ollie, forging a strong bond. As Ollie came into his own, he became both nephew and missing brother; he took his father's place. The three of them needed each other. It was beautiful to witness. I was very grateful that my son had men in the family to lean on. I had come to rely on them too. Scott was warm and funny and showed up when my brother died. Now we were all mourning Scott's loss, far too soon.

This gathering also honored my mother-in-law who had died not long after Scott. I believe she died of a broken heart. She had lost two sons, two grandsons, and her husband. If I had been in her place, I wouldn't have been able to go on either. She and I had a strained relationship after Jerry died. We hadn't been in touch for many years, but after Scott's death, I wrote to her. Ross told me how much she appreciated it.

The only scheduled event would be the burying of her ashes and her husband's in the family plot, next door to where her parents had lived. I remember being shocked and disoriented when Jerry brought me to meet his grandmother Nonny and his grandfather Boppy and walked me and our dog over to the cemetery adjacent to their yard. Years later, I wrote a play with a scene between two young lovers set in a cemetery. At the time, I told my husband-to-be that I wouldn't be buried there. He nodded, seeing the field of stone markers as if for the first time. A city girl, I felt alienated from the world that he had grown up in, but over the years, Nonny and her home became a source of stability and comfort. She was the only grandmother I had ever known, and I loved her.

Now, long after Jerry's death, my in-laws finally felt like family. A paradox. No single moment marked the shift. Instead, it seemed to be the very air we breathed together—our shared history—and it permeated every interaction that weekend. The change was unexpected, but the many years taken to reach this point didn't diminish its authenticity. When I was "Mrs. Mosier," though I never officially took his name, I didn't feel that I was part of this clan. (It didn't help that they called him "Mike," his middle name, and I called him Jerry, the first name he reclaimed in college.) Now, I did—a validation that I didn't know I craved. Although we didn't see or speak to each other often, we were undeniably kin.

In the brief graveside service, given by a minister and family friend, he acknowledged not only my parents-in-law, and Scott, but also, Jerry, though my husband had been buried a decade and a half earlier in our then hometown, Montclair, New Jersey. I was touched by the consideration.

For the rest of the weekend, we sat on the second-floor hotel porch overlooking Wyalusing's old-fashioned Main Street and told rambling stories about things past and present, reacquainting ourselves. At the last dinner in the hotel dining room, Ross and I wrangled over the check. I insisted, loudly, on treating everyone. My son and daughter-in-law seemed embarrassed at my brashness. I had grabbed Ross' credit card and replaced it with mine. The rest of the table laughed nervously, as I said, "I'm the oldest person here," as if my age conferred authority. My sister-in-law's husband asserted that *he* was the oldest. I pressed on, looking Ross in the eye. "It's what Jerry would have done. I'm standing in for him." I was twisting my brother-in-law's arm with a dose of manipulation, but why? Was I adamant that I should pay simply because that was my husband's modus operandi? No. There was more to it. Though I did indeed feel more a part of this family I had married into than ever before, there was a lingering sense that I needed to cement my status, even at this late date. Paying for the meal was a crude way of demonstrating that I belonged, but it was all I had. Ross nodded and I handed the card to the waitress.

Bill settled, we posed for a family photo and surrounded the hotel's pool table for a game. I wasn't much of pool player, though we'd had a pool table in our New Jersey home. Instead, I danced with my niece to the music blaring over the speakers, celebrating a sweet weekend, as I was wont to do, by moving to the beat.

For months leading up to the Minneapolis reunion, I thought more and more about the sister I expected to see again after so long: the on again, off again relationship we had had for years before the final break, which occurred by mutual decision shortly after our brother's death in 2011. He had been the middle child and as the tensions ebbed and flowed between his sisters, he became the glue that held us together. Once he was gone, the glue dissolved. She and I viewed our family quite differently, especially our mother. My sister believed that everything Mother did was right and my caveats regarding her behavior toward me were wrong, and worse, that I was to blame for each misstep Mother made. I loved my mother but understood that she had flaws, as we all do. My sister needed our mother to be infallible. Invariably, this was where any disagreement, even those about unrelated issues, landed. Eventually, after decades of this impasse, I decided to walk away; the cost to my peace of mind had become too great. My sister must have agreed, because she made no efforts towards reconciliation. Since then, I had learned to live without her and found sisterhood with my close friends and cousins.

In the end, the dreaded in-person sibling confrontation came to nothing. Two weeks before the reunion, my sister wrote to M that she wouldn't attend. I was relieved. Neither of us wanted *re*-union, because the *union* hadn't held in the first place. There was nothing left to reunite. Without such pain looming over the festivities, they could proceed as the three of us, the sister-cousins, had envisioned.

Summer 2024. Twenty descendants and their significant others gathered outside Grandmother Sophia's Minneapolis home, an immaculately maintained house that reminded us of an English cottage complete with lush garden and shady patio. We posed for a photo before its arched front door, gleaming white siding, and gabled roof. Then we entered, let in by the current owner's friend—the owner was away and had graciously allowed us the morning to walk through this essential part of our history.

We broke into two groups so as not to crowd each other. D, who had spent a great deal of her childhood there, led the tour. We took in the dark wood trim around every first-floor opening, the leaded glass decorative windows on either side of the fireplace, the columns and built-in bookshelves framing the staircase to the second floor, the telephone corner, and the enclosed sunroom, which had been a porch. One of my cousins showed me a photograph of my mother as a child, lounging there, absorbed in a book.

Upstairs, D showed us my mother's room—the only girl, she was also the only child to have her own room—including a little reading nook to the side of the door, that struck me as a calm and sweet oasis. As I was about to follow D out of the room, she turned and said, "No, you stay here alone for a while. Feel her presence." I did. I could sense the little girl who had tried hard to please her own mother, and often failed, but who had retained her creativity—she was an artist—even as she navigated her mother's moods, and I identified.

Afterwards, we thanked the woman who had let us in. What a gift to be able to experience where we came from in such an intimate and concrete manner. Grandmother's house was a house of memories: my eldest cousin had brought them to life.

That afternoon, we had lunch at Lake Harriett and watched intrepid M kayak around it. Then we went to the cemetery where our grandparents and great-grand-parents were buried. It was a summer afternoon and the bugs were out. Before we got to the grave site, a couple of my relatives noticed a red line extending up my left leg. When I looked down, I thought I must have gotten scratched by something, because it didn't feel itchy. Looking more closely, I saw a series of red bumps. Whatever had bitten me had a feast. A cousin gave me some Benadryl cream, and I stood on the pavement while everyone else walked through the grass to the graves. A young cousin took photos for me. (Somehow, I had become reunion photographer of record.) As I watched my relatives circling around the site, I thought about the Pennsylvania reunion a year earlier with its graveside service and thought, *reunions can unite both the living and the dead.*

Later that evening everyone met for the formal dinner that would cap our time together. My sister-cousins and I had chosen an "old Minneapolis" restaurant to capture the nostalgic atmosphere we wanted. We gathered in a private dining room around a U-shaped table. At the front of the room our California cousin had set up a screen to display a comprehensive slide show of the family history from our grandparents to the present. He had labored hours to organize the dozens of photos that we had each contributed and had captioned them with humor and style.

M acted as master of ceremonies. She introduced the evening by thanking everyone for being there. In an apt characterization, she described our family as "centrifugal;" despite the strong outward pull, we had somehow managed to return to the center to celebrate our abiding kinship. After dinner, the stories began. We had planned for each of the "elders," including three male cousins, to tell any family tale they wished to share. M read the childhood section from our Hollywood uncle's unpublished semi-autobiographical novel. The West Coast cousin said that while amassing the slide show, he had been moved at how bittersweet it was—so many gone too soon whose pictures looked down at us. He acknowledged each one, my husband and brother among them. His brother spoke about how proud we ought to be of our many accomplishments and breadth of talents.

D spoke about Grandmother, and I learned things I hadn't known. She was inescapably a woman of her time, with an eighth-grade education and great frustration at not having an outlet, other than her children, to fulfill her musical gifts and intelligence, as well as from the pressures of being a single parent at a time when divorce was rare and Jews in her neighborhood rarer. The isolation and financial strain must have been very difficult. No wonder she had explosive outbursts and was so tough on those around her.

My mother, the youngest child, had spent more time alone with Grandmother than any of her siblings. Locked together with little respite, they were hard on themselves and hard on each other—a way of treating those closest that continued into the home she built with my father.

I found myself thinking that it was too bad my sister couldn't hear D tell Sophia's story. She might have recognized the undeniable link between our mother, our grandmother, and ourselves. Mother had called me "too dramatic," whenever I had a crying jag as a teenager. I called her "judgmental." Now, I understand that these behaviors were familial. The cost of all this unprocessed history and emotion had produced serious rifts between and within generations. We were both our mother's daughters and had more in common than we could acknowledge to each other. Sadly, what we had in common also kept us apart.

When it was my turn to speak, I stood and read the brief remarks I had written:

> "I'm beyond happy that this cousins' reunion has happened. Years ago, when I said something wistful in passing in a phone conversation with D about wishing we could bring everyone together, I wasn't sure how that would be possible, but with the determination and strength of my sister-cousins it has! And in the home city where so much of our history began. Thank you for being here.
>
> My story isn't about meeting Grandmother. I never had that opportunity. I spoke with her on the phone once and remember a

lively, lilting voice, but that's all. When at nine or ten, I asked my mother why I hadn't met her mother, she said—brace yourself—"Because I can't handle it."

(My cousins laughed in recognition.)

At that time, I didn't understand her answer, but of course, I do now. Bristly relationships are a thing on our side of the family. I was a teenager when Grandmother died, and the door closed for good. *Or did it?*

Today was actually the second time I'd been in Grandmother's house. The first was twenty-one years ago, when Jerry and I took Oliver on a midwestern college tour. (Ollie sends his regrets for not being able to be here.) We went to Carleton, where Mother had wanted to go, but didn't, and to Macalester. Ollie ended up at the University of Chicago, another family institution, but I've never regretted that weekend in Minneapolis.

D must have given us the address, because next thing I knew, we were on the street, parked in our rental car in front of Grandmother's house. Jerry was nothing if not bold. "Let's see if they'll let us in." He knocked on the door and they did. It was extraordinary. I imagined my mother as a little girl running up and down the staircase.

Afterwards, as we left the house, a neighbor waved us over. The woman must have heard us talking (windows open). She smiled and said, "I knew your grandmother, and I remember your mother." This neighbor must have been a child then. She went on to tell us that she remembered what a fine dresser Grandmother was in her beautifully tailored suits, and what a good singing voice she had—something Mother and my cousins confirmed.

It was a delight to hear such a first-hand account that afternoon, just as it is being here with you, seeing our ancestors in your faces, hearing them in your voices, bringing them to life in a profoundly rewarding way.

(Then I choked up.) Today, the door that closed for me when Grandmother died, opened."

After the weight of what their elders had to say sank in, it took the second cousins—the next generation—time to muster the nerve to speak, but they did, movingly expressing their gratitude to us. We sat for one more group photo, holding up the sepia place cards of Grandmother Sophia as a beautiful eighteen-year-old.

As we said our goodbyes, one of my cousins told me that he never knew that our grandparents had divorced; his father had never talked about it. I told him that my mother had taken the opposite approach, talking endlessly about the shame of divorce and how, no matter what, she wouldn't repeat it. So many missing pieces, some of them basic, that were put back into the puzzle of our upbringing simply by coming together in person. Then I said that I thought the weekend had been "healing." He smiled and nodded. I felt deep satisfaction at the success of this warm and meaningful reunion.

These four reunions revealed much: one moment of past meets present at Interlochen, a celebratory dance at Vassar, an assertion of belonging in Pennsylvania, and a long-awaited gathering of far-flung generations in Minnesota affirmed both change and continuity, the threads, loose yet enduring, that tied me to classmates and family. I thought about the centrifugal nature of each reunited group; we had been flung together and could be flung apart. I didn't know when or whether we would see each other again, but I knew with certainty that our connection would remain.

Stuffing

I think of my mother a lot these days, ever since I passed an age she never reached. Reminiscence, however, can't surpass the pleasure of preparing her recipe for stuffing every Thanksgiving. Then memories of her flood in, undiluted by our complicated history.

Six a.m.: nutmeg and onions wafting up the stairs and into my childhood bedroom. I'd roll over, pulling the Hudson Bay blanket over my head, breathing in my own sleepy scent. A couple more hours, I'd tell myself. The resolve to sleep lasted a nanosecond and off the covers would go. The smell was too enticing to resist. Up and out, I'd bound, into the kitchen to offer myself as sous chef to my mother's "master."

She never accepted help, at least not in the kitchen.

"Set the table," she'd say.

And every November, I would dutifully comply— spreading the blue and green Provençal tablecloth, gathering the white cloth napkins, and good silver ladles with the signature Jensen handles, the Wedgwood platters with their bas-relief scenes, and the Waterford crystal bowls we used only once a year for cranberry sauce and for the pickled onions no one ever touched. We didn't have a complete set of anything, but somehow our mismatched best looked festive enough.

Thanksgiving was my mother's favorite holiday. "No religion. Lots of food," she'd declare.

But just because it was free of oppressive institutional ritual didn't mean it was easy. For all the celebratory clinking of eggnog mugs—virgin for the children, spiked for the adults—as we watched Macy's parade transform from black and white to color on our ever larger television sets, all those giddy freezing spectators clad in layers of wool and multiple scarves long before *Polartec* trimmed their collective silhouettes, for all the *aren't we lucky, here we are warm and safe, and soon to be fed*, dinner itself could be a tense affair. We tried our darndest to be cheery and properly appreciative even when awkward discomfort inserted itself.

Mother wasn't much of a cook. Most of her dishes were rather dull. She didn't like to bake, so the pies were store-brought with an artificial aftertaste in the too-thick crust. If she could have gotten away with it, she would have boiled the turkey, like her old-standby, Jewish Mama chicken.

But there was one dish she was known for, and that was her stuffing. Her stuffing was extraordinary. As far as we were concerned, it *was* Thanksgiving. My brother, sister, and I would watch, wiping sleepy crud from our eyes as Mother packed the last of her scrumptious mixture into the bird and closed its opening, which resembled a cave blocked by the landslide of half an apple. For the next several hours, as she opened and closed the oven door to baste the turkey, we'd salivate over the hearty, sweet and savory, herb-heavy concoction.

Though my mother had no real interest in the culinary arts, she put her considerable creativity into the stuffing; the rest went into her paintings—bold abstract watercolors on large pieces of rough Italian paper—and, of course, her children. Dinner guests speculated. *Was it the celery, the raisins, or the allspice that gave the mush its distinctive flavor?* Though I watched her prepare, getting up earlier and earlier to witness the process, I could never quite absorb the steps, but I was certain that the combination of sage, fruit, chestnuts, butter, broth, and ordinary *Pepperidge Farm* bread mix was the most satisfying blend I'd ever tasted.

Year after year, the stuffing got us through many less-than-perfect holiday meals. Whatever was happening at the table dissipated as soon as our tongues lapped up its moist, rich yumminess. Whether it was my brother's first drink at the age of ten after which he passed out on the sofa, or my sister's meltdown at thirteen over one of my blunt assessments of her dubious sanity, or the reluctant inclusion of my fiancé into the proceedings, during which my parents glared at each other instead of the intruder, everyone dug into seconds and thirds of Mother's stuffing.

That's what we came back for, again and again.

When, in her final six months, Mother could no longer eat, except through a tube in her stomach, she still insisted, over our futile objections, on cooking one last Thanksgiving dinner. After the preparation was done, she sat enthroned at the end of the dining table, breathing through her tracheotomy tube, thirty pounds lighter than the Thanksgiving before, and watched us eat. None of us, except my seven-year-old son, had an appetite. In unison, we moved fork to mouth, glass to lips. My father didn't lift his eyes from his plate. But the one dish we devoured was the stuffing. Between huge helpings—we knew this was the last time she would prepare it—we smiled at her and said in an overlapping chorus, "Great stuffing, Mom."

Thirty years later, I still serve my mother's stuffing. So much has changed. There are the losses, those missing from the table: my father, my husband, my brother, and of course, Mother herself. The setting has morphed from our first marital apartment in Park Slope, Brooklyn, to our tiny first house in Montclair, New Jersey, then a bigger one in the same town, where we would sit at the dining table that had been my parents', and finally, in the past ten years, at that same table in my lakeside Hudson Valley home.

Hosting Thanksgiving has become especially gratifying in my reinvented life—the sheer continuity of it. The contrast between this holiday and others throughout the year strikes especially strongly now that I live alone, because Thanksgiving means family togetherness. It is still what it always was—a warm occasion of shared food, love, and gratitude. My sister-in-law Jeanne, my niece and nephew Leo and Isabel, come every year, bearing wine and pie, and lately, their dog, a bouncing Labradoodle named Bugbee. With Tizzie, my yellow lab, gone, I get my "dog fix" from Bugbee's visits. Some years, Jerry's siblings bring their families.

Everyone pitches in. Leo does the cranberry sauce and Isabel chops the herbs. My husband taught our son knife skills, to my alarmed objections, when Ollie was a kindergartener. No accidents then or now. He has become master of the side dishes, from traditional mashed potatoes to sautéed Brussel sprouts to beet salad. His wife, Christina, takes charge of the sweet potatoes. I handle the turkey and stuffing, as well as a breakfast pumpkin cake that has become an expected staple.

At first, it was difficult to achieve the cohesion of taste and textures, the nutty and the succulent, that said Thanksgiving to us all. Over the past three decades, every so often, I'd try something new—sausage and sage perhaps, or cornbread instead of a mixed herb base. But inevitably, I would return to the stuffing of my childhood. I've added touches of my own—cherries in addition to raisins, shallots instead of onions, but the essence of Mother's dish remains. The act of preparing it—chopping the celery, sautéing the mushroom, melting the butter, inhaling a time past—brings me closer to her. Whatever scuffles we had—and there were many—they paled next to the power of this one dish. I am grateful for her recipe, which revives her in its taste, aroma, and in yearly anticipation. I conjure my mother through a shake of nutmeg and a pinch of salt and thank her for this dish. And for everything else. Yes, everything—the ways she championed my creative life, as well as her disappointing coolness regarding my personal one—because it all blended into my resiliency and self-knowledge. Though I didn't always like her, I loved her, and I knew her—what she approved and disapproved of—and therefore I knew myself, what to push for and what to push against. I came from this talented, opinionated woman, and identified with her artistic tastes, and this delectable culinary one. Each November, I am happily anchored as I re-create her earthiest gift.

Mother didn't deign to give me the recipe until I was grown and hosting my own holiday dinners. I've given it out only to close family. Until now. Happy Thanksgiving!

Mother's Stuffing

For a 12-to-16-pound turkey

1 bag *Pepperidge Farm* seasoned
   stuffing
1 stick unsalted butter
2 ½ cups water
¾ -1 cup sliced morel mushrooms
Extra virgin olive oil
4 celery stalks, chopped
½ apple, chopped
½ apple, whole

½ cup yellow raisins
½ cup red raisins or currants
1 cup dried cherries
1 cup chopped chestnuts (optional)
1 cup sherry
½ cup onions, chopped
dash of nutmeg, allspice, cloves,
   mace
1 T each finely chopped fresh sage,
   rosemary, and thyme

Follow the directions on the stuffing bag by melting 1 stick of butter with 2 ½ cups of water. Put stuffing in a large bowl; add melted butter. Sauté mushrooms in olive oil and butter; add chopped celery and onions to sauté. When onions and celery are soft, add to stuffing, along with the mushrooms. Finely chop the fresh sage, rosemary, and thyme. Add to stuffing. Pour in sherry and mix well. Stir in yellow and red raisins, cherries, chopped apple, and chestnuts (if desired). Add a dash of nutmeg, allspice, cloves, and mace. Stir until well mixed. Stuff turkey, front and back, and close front opening with ½ apple. For vegetarian guests, you may bake a portion of the stuffing separately in an oven proof dish at 350 degrees for 40 minutes.

Hudson Valley Happiness

When I moved from my long-time home in New Jersey to the Hudson Valley, friends and family expressed concern. "How will you get along without people who know you?" they asked.

I answered, "By introducing myself, of course." And that's what I've done. I admit that I, too, had some misgivings prior to the move, but I wouldn't have taken such a plunge if I hadn't thought—*known*—that I would be okay, that I would meet people, make new friends.

And I have.

It's true that one can't make old friends. Those are irreplaceable. Camp song lyrics run around and around in my head: *Make new friends, but the keep the old/ One is silver, the other gold.* There's nothing like shared histories and the stories we know about each other by heart. When an old friend enters my new home, she recognizes elements from a past we shared; when a new friend enters, the house and its contents introduce them to who I am. Even so, it was reassuringly easy to get to know my lakeside neighbors, as well as book group members from surrounding towns, and to become part of the Rhinebeck Rotarians.

From day one, my neighbors began introducing themselves. One sauntered up my driveway with her little girl, who presented me with daisies. "Welcome," they said. I was a mess, having just presided over six hours of movers carrying all my worldly possessions into my new house. It hardly mattered. When I accepted the flowers from the small, outstretched hand, I felt embraced by this new community. In the days following, as I walked my dog around the road, which circled Shooks Pond, our spring-fed twelve and a half acres of paradise, I met more people. When I went swimming for the first time, on the Fourth of July, I introduced myself to the others in the association—some weekenders, some full time, some who only show up to swim, because they never built a house on their plot of land, some, my age, who had spent every summer there since childhood. I envied such continuity and was thankful to be accepted by the lake's "old guard," simply because I loved being there as much as they did.

Within weeks, a few of the women and I had dinner at my place—my first dinner party. I dubbed us "The Ladies of the Lake," and we decided then and there to meet regularly to gab and enjoy each other's company. Our histories seeped out. They knew that I was a widow, but that didn't cast a shadow over our encounters. They saw me as I was in the present: healed and eager to start over in such a beautiful setting.

The ease of meeting people here may have had something to do with the intimate nature of the local villages, but I believe that it also reflected a change within myself. The hardships of the previous years had broken me open. As a result, I drank in new experiences, and welcomed new people into my life, and they in turn welcomed me.

When my first memoir came out, the Ladies of the Lake showed up at my local reading and signing. They celebrated with me at the after-party I threw at the restaurant next door. After reading the book, they held a book group discussion to share their thoughts. They were generous in their support. I felt seen and respected.

Over time, relationships shifted and changed. Women I thought would become my closest friends drifted away or left the scene altogether, and others, who weren't such early candidates, proved true blue. It took multiple engagements to share enough about each other with each other to cement a bond. That no one I met knew me as a married woman, or as an actress—previously central identities—and that no one could know my husband sometimes struck me as strange. But in fact, Jerry, our marriage, and my past creative life were layered into the person I'd become, and for my new friends that seemed to be knowledge enough.

Spring in the Hudson Valley is announced by the sound of the peepers, tiny chorus frogs that chirp together at night, just as the weather warms. Their piping is so penetrating that at first I was tempted to close my balcony doors, so the choir wouldn't keep me awake. But I quickly decided that the cacophony, along with the breeze, were welcome. How delightful that these small creatures could herald the changing season. Peep on!

A gopher lived under my tool shed. He was big and fat and fast on his feet—very fast for one so broad and thick. I would have thought that he would lumber rather than race when I opened the back door and caught him grazing near the hostas, but at the sound of the latch unlocking, he was off. My dog, too, could send him running. One bark and the gopher would jump. No large, shedding, domesticated canine would ever get him.

Tizzie, my yellow lab, didn't know that, of course. She watched the backyard intently, nose to the screen of the dog-level casement windows, sniffing the fresh summer air for signs of wildlife, ready to lunge at Mr. Gopher, the chipmunks who scattered at her bark, or the rabbit family who lived yards from the shed under the brush along the over-grown pond waters behind my home. The rabbits worked front and back, a pattern that forced me to put a gate in front of the sunroom doors, lest Tizzie ram the glass door at the sight of a cottontail nibbling under my lawn table. When she went outside to sniff around, all the critters retreated. She rolled in the grass, rubbing her back on the animal-scented ground, ecstatic.

My first two winters in the Hudson Valley were harsher than most by all reports—unusually cold and icy. Hungry deer boldly lunched on my front holly bushes. I knocked at the front windows to scare them off, but they stared me down, as if to say, "I dare you to keep me away." I tried to go with the flow, thinking, *at least there'll be no need to trim in the spring.*

In the New Jersey suburb where I last resided, there were gophers, rabbits, and endless deer sleeping on my front lawn. Once, during a beastly hot summer, a mother left her two fawns all day under the shade of a locust tree, three feet from my front steps. The postman walked by them, and they barely lifted their little heads. I dubbed it my deer day care center. But the feeling of living alongside nature was more profound, more spiritual here than it was in semi-urban Montclair. The connection between ground, sky, and water, between tree, bush, and flower was less controlled and for that reason, more enveloping. In Montclair, residents considered the geese in Edgemont Park a nuisance, but here, I counted them and marveled. When only a few showed up, I worried.

One morning in late August, I was up earlier than usual and looked out my kitchen window to see an army of geese marching down the lake road. There were so many that I thought I was hallucinating. All summer I had enjoyed the comings and goings of a family of geese: a mother, a father, and one, two, or three goslings. At one point, the mother had been nesting on the edge of the road and squawked wildly when Tizzie and I walked past. I had worried when, a little while later, I saw that the nest had been destroyed and found pieces of eggshell crushed on the pavement. Then I witnessed a kind of grieving: mother and father alone on the water, aimlessly circling—I imagined, bereft. But I had never seen more than six or seven geese together.

Until that morning.

I began to count. Twenty-eight. There were twenty-eight geese walking down the road. The number was startling, as was the behavior. Usually they ate grass lakeside, walked the water's perimeter, or swam. They didn't take to the pavement. I studied them a while longer and then went back to my bedroom to get ready for the day. When I returned, all traces of the flock had vanished. The water was still, the sky pale blue and uninhabited, and the road empty. I missed them. I wanted them back.

I didn't golf. Never had. Never would, even though my community was adjacent to a semi-private golf course. Every day for the first few years in my new home, I walked my dog around our lake road and passed the sweeping greens of the Red Hook Golf Club, admiring the evergreens dotting the grounds. The sky overhead seemed particularly vast and clear as it framed the gently rolling course. I marveled at the pillowy cumulus clouds above it and the vivid sunsets on its horizon as I strolled west in the early evening.

In the morning, Tizzie and I would nod to the groundskeepers riding by on their large mowing machines. The lake association and the golf club had an agreement that allowed the club to drive on our road to maintain its property. I never tired of walking by the well-manicured course with my girl trotting alongside. In the afternoon, we watched the golf carts making their way along the paths between holes. Sometimes, we waved—my hand, her tail—if its occupants were close enough. When a golfer stepped down to scope out his or her next shot, we held our greetings—Tizzie somehow knew not to bark—respectful of the concentration necessary to advance in this seemingly impossible game.

My second September here marked my first as a member of the Rhinebeck Rotary Club, and my first as a volunteer for their annual Golf Classic, a yearly fundraiser. I had never been much of a joiner, but the need to meet people prompted me to do something my husband would have done—join a community service group. The Rhinebeck Rotary motto, "Service Above Self," sounded promising. I was pleased to find that the Rotary membership wasn't only businessmen, but men and women from a variety of professions, including the arts. The Rotary brought people and opportunities into my life. Through the Rotary, I met the head of the local theater, who produced my shows and became a dear friend, as well as other interesting people—photographers, psychologists, producers, financial planners, and attorneys—who became friends too. The weekly meetings anchored my calendar and their invited speakers, often from outside the group, taught me about the area's history and current concerns. The Rotary gave me a way to quickly understand the villages I was now part of and the means to give back.

The Golf Classic brought my two worlds together. Many of my lake neighbors participated. It seemed that those who had been in the community the longest were avid golfers, and those who, like me, had bought homes more recently, were there for the quiet and the water. Luckily, I didn't have to know anything about golf to collect raffle tickets or to greet the golfers at the second hole and monitor their shots. This was the Hole-in-One location, with a very handsome silver and black Jeep on display. Anyone making the shot would win a two-year lease for the car, which had been donated by a local car dealership. In the more than twenty-year history of the tournament no one had ever won. My partner and I, armed with binoculars trained on the hole's blue flag, were charged with verifying the shots. One player came within a foot of the hole, another two within a yard. Watching the concentration and skill involved in even making it onto the green, confirmed that golf wasn't for me. I was patient in many aspects of my life, but the long slow trek through eighteen holes would drive me crazy. My tolerance for the elusive would stay firmly in the world of the arts.

No matter. As fall approached, I looked forward with great anticipation to the reds, golds, and flaming oranges of the deciduous trees along the perimeter of the golf course, to the first carpet of snow in December, and to the peace it offered as my dog and I walked together. After Tizzie died, I walked alone—not every day, though I vowed as much during her last weeks—but often. The landscape comforted me; seasonal change was predictable, natural. Leaves fall. Dogs die. The land, my dear girl, and I were all part of the endless cycle.

My late husband introduced me to the serenity of kayaking, though his kayak adventures were more intrepid than mine. Jerry had accompanied marathon swimmers around the island of Manhattan and thought nothing of sea kayaking in the Atlantic during our vacations on Martha's Vineyard. He taught our seven-year-old to kayak, and he taught me. Ollie, now in his late thirties, has been kayaking for thirty years, and like his dad was confident enough to tackle any kind of waterway. I preferred the protected quiet of a lake or pond to the roughness of an ocean or sound. I needed to know that I could swim to shore in five minutes or less. By that standard, Shooks Pond was perfect.

Jerry was also an advertising writer. When he started his own company, he sought out clients who mirrored his interests, and landed *Perception*, one of the better-known kayak manufacturers. His passion for their product had won them over. Ollie and I have copies of his ads on our walls: "the alternative to a workout that doesn't go anywhere." Sometimes he got paid in kayaks. After his death, I sold the largest one, as well as a collapsible version, that I couldn't assemble. Ollie kept another at a friend's house in Connecticut, and I stored the purple child-sized kayak on which Ollie learned to kayak, for a potential grandchild.

When I heard that the lake's ubiquitous lily pads were being treated in keeping with the New York Department of Environmental Conservation's standards, I realized that once they were under control, I would be able to "put in" just steps from my driveway and resolved to purchase a kayak of my own. For my sixty-second birthday, I bought myself a present: an L.L. Bean *Manatee* in lime green. Alone at the beach or on the water in my kayak, I had the feeling that the pond was mine, all mine.

I imagined that Bob Shook, whose family owned this pond and all the acreage around it before parceling out the property in 1926 to create our homeowners association, felt that way too, when he took his seven-a.m. daily swim throughout the spring, summer, and right up until the frost. But, of course, he'd had his name on it. I would watch him from my kitchen windows while I drank my morning coffee, thankful as the weather got colder, not to be him, but reassured by his regular presence. When Bob died suddenly a few years ago, the community gathered in his yard high above the lake for a memorial and send-off. We looked down at the water as his family paddled Bob's swimming route and scattered his ashes along the way.

As I glided the perimeter of the pond and crossed through its deeper middle passage, a sense of well-being enveloped me. The sun bounced off the smooth surface. A heron alighted on a diving platform. A neighbor waved. I was alone, yet fully part of my community of water-lovers. I paddled on, grateful for the relaxation and peace that the lake afforded me.

Though I loved watching the many geese who walked the road in front of my house, no one who lived around the lake liked the poop that covered the floating raft, which had been meant for swimmers to rest and sun, if only it were clean. One day, after two of my neighbors re-anchored the platform to the center of the lake—it had drifted during the winter—we discussed

the issue. One of the men told me that they had tried various solutions—a scarecrow of sorts, which had quickly disintegrated, lights which didn't discourage geese from landing—but nothing had worked.

"Why not post a decoy predator on the corner of the platform?" I suggested. Next thing I knew, they had placed a "scare owl" on the raft, a realistic bird about a foot high, whose head swiveled in the wind. Success! No goose droppings on it since.

At the end-of-summer beach picnic, my neighbor told me that they had named it "Roselee the Owl." I whooped. They had no idea how central owls were to my personal mythology. I collect them in ceramic form, on dishes, and posters. As a teen, I created a vivid persona for a stuffed owl to entertain my siblings; the character lasted well into adulthood and diffused many a marital argument. I laughed and said, "My work here is done. I've left my mark on Shooks Pond."

I can't say my happiness in the Hudson Valley has been undiluted, however, I *can* say it has been my baseline, my default state, if you will. *How sad or bad can anything be when every day I look out my kitchen windows at a lake, lush greenery, geese, rabbits, ducks, chipmunks, the occasional heron, and the glorious sky?* Not very. Not too. Sadness has only been a brief unwanted guest here, though it was my constant companion in the years before I moved. Mostly, I am content—in a word, happy. What does that mean exactly? I sleep well most nights, although occasionally, if I have binge-watched too much political news or hit the pillow making mental lists of the next day's chores, I'll be up until four a.m. I enjoy my daily solitary routine, even without a dog to shape it. I enjoy my freedom.

A therapist once told me that, "freedom is a huge responsibility." True. Freedom involves choices, which may appear luxurious to some, because frankly, they are. I'm free to do whatever I want whenever I want, because I'm a retired person of means. I am lucky. But the responsibility means that every decision is mine and mine alone, and that can be challenging, despite my advantages. Still, I'm healthy, creative, and feel acknowledged for my accomplishments as never before. I used to try hard to be seen, but unlike many women my age, I felt more visible in my sixties than ever before, partly because of literary recognition, but more likely because I finally saw and valued myself, and that became a source of deep satisfaction, and yes, happiness.

Change is the one certainty in life. Accepting that, I stepped into a new setting for my final chapter—the one Jane Fonda called "prime time." In so doing, I found renewal and perspective. Moving to this beautiful part of New York State twelve years ago marked the beginning of a "new me," the "After Jerry" me. At the time, I couldn't have understood how different my daily existence would become, but I knew in my bones that it would be good and right for this stage in my life. I trusted myself and took the leap. The out-of-the-ashes transformations that followed formed a living and rewarding sequel to the life I had led before. Just as traveling to Dubai and back was both a literal journey and a metaphor for traversing grief, the Hudson Valley became both my physical home and a symbol of inner contentment.

My home is filled with meaning, with talismans of past and present. The paintings and photographs on my walls, the folk art on my shelves, the pillows on my sofas, and the eclectic furniture throughout the space map the life I've led. All the homes I've lived in—from the red brick house of my childhood to my first apartment to the homes I shared with my husband and son—are reflected in the lake house. Though I live by myself, I am never truly alone in my home, because it is full of history that grounds me.

That said, to quote Stephen Pinker, "Happy people live in the present." I don't always manage it, but while I was painting the fence that separates me from my next-door neighbors, I realized that the project made me inordinately happy, perhaps because it involved pure present action. I don't love routine upkeep, but give me a one-time project to focus on and I'm in heaven. I love simple physical tasks that with a bit of sweat can achieve a desired effect. My neighbors had kindly painted the fence for me, but it matched their home (beige), not mine (gray). After a year of living with the result, I decided to rectify the situation by painting alternate sections of my side either the gray of my house or the gray of my shed-front steps-balcony. The subtle but distinctive shift in shades would give this rather ordinary fence a bit of panache. I felt motivated and energized, starting in the early morning, before the sun's heat baked me and the fence. Without any sounds in my ears other than the buzzing of the occasional bee and the drone of a biplane from the Rhinebeck Aerodrome overhead—I'd deliberately left my phone indoors—I slapped gray paint over beige slats, one by one, taking care to cover the edges without dripping onto the neighbor's side. The repetitive action of dipping my brush and swishing it up and down freed my mind. I could mull over stalled writing issues without getting stuck, because I had a job to do. After finishing each section, I would take a few steps back and admire my work. It looked good.

Who knew that such a mundane project would give me so much pleasure? Well, I guess I knew. And that's the beauty of being in my eighth decade. I can make myself happy with whatever or whomever is in front of me—a fencepost to paint, a lake to kayak, geese to watch, or a person to talk with. It doesn't take much.

As I was prepping the fence by trimming the weeds and vines overtaking it, I had a full-circle moment. A mother and her little daughter were walking around the road. They waved, and I motioned for them to come up my driveway. We chatted and the little girl handed me the small bouquet of wildflowers she had picked.

"No, no, you should keep them," I said.

"No, Roselee," the child said. She had met me on the beach the previous month, when the three of us were the only people swimming. "They're for you." She beamed a firm smile. The little girl wasn't going to take "no" for an answer.

I took the flowers, thanked her and flashed back to the mother and daughter who came up my driveway to give me daisies from their garden the day I moved in. That little girl is a teenager today. A child with a bouquet in her outstretched hand made me happy then, as it does now.

I used to rush ahead and get only so far. Now, letting go of the pressure to perform and to produce has brought me more inner freedom than I've ever known. I don't have to live up to anything anymore. I lead a quiet life, a good life. Now, pleasure in small present moments is everything. I can say with assurance that life doesn't get better than this.

Acknowledgments

I'd like to give special thanks to my dear son and daughter-in-law, Oliver and Christina, who allowed me to write about their wedding in "Best Day" and for the use of his remarks in that essay.

My great thanks to the publishing team who made this collection of personal essays possible: Director Kevin Atticks, who has championed my work from the beginning; developmental editor Olivia DiTroia for her astute review of the manuscript; and to the Apprentice House Press design team for their creativity and attention to detail.

And finally, I send much love and gratitude to my friends and family, the central people in my life, who will never be relegated to the periphery.

About the Author

Roselee Blooston is the author of the novel *Trial by Family*, a Gold Medal Winner in the 2020 Independent Publisher Book Awards, the memoir *Dying in Dubai*, a 2016 Foreword INDIES Book of the Year Winner and a 2017 Eric Hoffer Award Finalist, the collection *The Chocolate Jar and Other Stories* (2022), and the memoir *Almost: My Life in the Theater* (2022)—all published by Apprentice House Press. Her plays have been produced nationally and internationally, including over *Voice of America*. Other publications include *AARP The Magazine*, literary journals, and anthologies—among them, *The Widows' Handbook*. She founded the non-profit Tunnel Vision Writers' Project, taught in university programs, and currently coaches and edits privately. She lives in Red Hook, New York. For more information go to *www. roseleeblooston.com*

Apprentice
House Press
Loyola University Maryland

Apprentice House is the country's only campus-based, student-staffed book publishing company. Directed by professors and industry professionals, it is a nonprofit activity of the Communication Department at Loyola University Maryland.

Using state-of-the-art technology and an experiential learning model of education, Apprentice House publishes books in untraditional ways. This dual responsibility as publishers and educators creates an unprecedented collaborative environment among faculty and students, while teaching tomorrow's editors, designers, and marketers.

Outside of class, progress on book projects is carried forth by the AH Book Publishing Club, a co-curricular campus organization supported by Loyola University Maryland's Office of Student Activities.

Eclectic and provocative, Apprentice House titles intend to entertain as well as spark dialogue on a variety of topics. Financial contributions to sustain the press's work are welcomed. Contributions are tax deductible to the fullest extent allowed by the IRS.

To learn more about Apprentice House books or to obtain submission guidelines, please visit www.apprenticehouse.com.

Apprentice House
Communication Department
Loyola University Maryland
4501 N. Charles Street
Baltimore, MD 21210
410-617-5265
info@apprenticehouse.com
www.apprenticehouse.com